# CIVIL WAR
# ON WESTERN WATERS

# CIVIL WAR

## on

# WESTERN WATERS

*by*

FLETCHER PRATT

*Illustrated with Maps and Photographs*

HENRY HOLT AND COMPANY

NEW YORK

87174-0216

Printed in the United States of America

# Contents

# Introduction

WHEN THE Civil War began with the firing on Fort Sumter, early on the morning of April 12, 1861, it was clear that there were entailed the most serious economic consequences for the Northwest; the states of the old Northwest Territory—Ohio, Indiana, Illinois, Michigan, Wisconsin—with the newer Iowa, Minnesota, and at least the northern part of Missouri. Their products were lumber, corn, wheat, fruit, meat, and the by-products of these, and the normal route by which they reached their markets was the Mississippi. A good part of these products was absorbed by the Southern cotton plantations; the remainder was transshipped for Europe at New Orleans. A not inconsiderable part of Southern cotton passed north by the same river route. The railroads had begun to carry northwestern products to the eastern seaboard, but they had not yet attained anywhere near the importance of the river traffic. Water transportation is always cheaper.

It was this economic exchange quite as much as geography that led Lincoln to pronounce in his first inaugural: "Physically speaking, we cannot separate." And it was this economic exchange that offered the most obvious point of attack. The Civil War had other causes than the economic, but in the west, throughout the Mississippi system, its purpose in the beginning was the exertion of economic pressure. In effect, the South said: "We will blockade the river; now let us see you dispose of your goods," and the North replied: "We will blockade the river; now what are you going to do for the goods you need?"

As the text will show, the high contending parties had quite different ideas about the methods by which these blockades were to be achieved. The important thing to note at present is that there had never been a warship on the rivers, except for some small craft below New Orleans during the War of 1812. Not only was the whole science of naval architecture in a state of flux at this time, due to the introduction of steam, iron armor, and several new types of guns, but also the rivers imposed special limitations, such as shallow draft and great handiness for getting around bends. Everything was to improvise, everything was to make, everything to combine out of various and often incompatible elements.

In the area of construction, that is. In the field of strategy it was very early discovered that the rivers, in the words of Mahan about the ocean, were "not a barrier, but a highway," giving incomparable logistic advantage to the side that held them. The thing that gave the war on western waters its peculiar character is that "control of the sea" could not be won in battle and then held; it had to be constantly reaffirmed. After Trafalgar, the British fleet was immune to any force that could be brought against it; the Union river navy had to do as much fighting at the end of the war as at the beginning, and it was as difficult. Moreover, there was always an ulterior purpose; nothing could be done from purely naval considerations.

The river war thus deserves the abused adjective "unique"; there has never been anything like it, and it is highly unlikely there ever will be. Also, it played a vital part in the outcome of the Civil War of which it was a branch. It is therefore rather surprising that the data on it have never before been assembled in one place. In the 1880's Admiral (then Commander) Mahan did produce a short book called *The Gulf and Inland Waters* as one of a series, but he looked upon Mississippi operations with a seaman's eye as more or less appendictical to what was happening in the Gulf blockade, and he lacked not only many personal memoirs that have since come to light but even the official records. This is not to criticize Mahan, who wrote the book he was asked to write, full of wisdom and insight, but to indicate that he was not aware of the full story and, under the conditions, could not be.

The river war was so closely interwoven with the military campaigns that it has been necessary to say something about the latter to make episodes comprehensible, but every effort has been made to hold this down to a minimum. Indeed, one cannot go very far into the material without discovering that the Confederate concept of holding the rivers was primarily military, from the banks, the way rivers are held in Europe, while almost from the beginning the Union idea was naval, or at least amphibious. But that is a matter for the text.

Some details need annotation. Both Union and Confederacy, confronted with a naval war in which everything had to be improvised, adopted all sorts of expedients, and this appears nowhere more sharply than in the rankings of emergency officers. It is not at all uncommon to find in the records names preceded by such locutions as "Acting Volunteer Master's Mate" or "Acting Volunteer Lieutenant-Commander," which is to say that the origin as well as the nature of a man's rank was indicated by his official title. In the text these cumbersome titles have been cut

down to size by the omission of "Acting" and "Volunteer."
A "Volunteer Lieutenant" was theoretically outranked by
a regular "Lieutenant" and in turn outranked an "Acting
Volunteer Lieutenant," but in practice it was a question
of who was in charge of what job, and the additions to the
titles are mere verbal decoration.

A "Master" of Civil War days would rank about with a
first-class warrant today; he took a salute but had no
commission, and when in charge of a ship carried the
courtesy title of "Captain." The rank of "Ensign" began
to appear in the Union navy in 1863, usually with "Acting"
attached; he was below a "Master." There may have been
midshipmen in the river navies, but there is no discernible
record of them. All ranks on the rivers were relatively
very low; the only captain (by rank) on the Union side was
Pennock, and Phelps and Fitch, with as many as 12 ships
under their command, were only lieutenant commanders.

It has been necessary to give some of the administrative
history of the Confederate Navy Department to make
events comprehensible. This is not true of the Union
operations, so the story of Mr. Welles and his assistants
has been left to a place where they more clearly belong.

# CIVIL WAR
# ON WESTERN WATERS

# 1

# Rally Round the Flag, Boys

Opening scene: St. Louis, Missouri, in an atmosphere charged with heat and the promise of thunder. The telegrams from Sumter were not two weeks old; still younger was Governor Jackson's bold defiance of Lincoln's call for troops—"Illegal, unconstitutional and revolutionary in its objects; inhuman and diabolical," Jackson called it, declaring Missouri would not furnish a man for the "unholy crusade." His State Militia under General D. M. Frost were drilling in the grove of Camp Jackson; the belles of St. Louis all came out to wave handkerchiefs at their knights, as they marched and countermarched through the fine spring weather.

Only one little flaw kept it from being true pageant; the guns that the knights swung so valorously to their shoulders were of wood, and the genuine fire-spitting weapons they should have had were in the St. Louis arsenal, guarded

by a red-bearded captain from Connecticut and some companies of German immigrants, togged out as home guards.
Of course, the knights regarded the situation as imperma-
nent, if intolerable; Governor Jackson had sent emissaries
to Jefferson Davis, president of the new Confederacy of the
South, to tell him that if he wished another star in his flag,
he had better furnish some of the physical means for placing it there. The wires said a steamboat full of rifles was on
the way up from Baton Rouge; when they come we shall
see what will happen to the "swine swept from the German
gutters."

We shall see—and as tension mounted in the streets and
on the levees, in homes and in churches, a retired businessman named James B. Eads was reading a letter:

Be not surprised if you are called here suddenly by telegram.
If called, come instantly. In a certain contingency it will be
necessary to have the aid of the most thorough knowledge of
our Western Rivers and the use of steam on them, and in that
event I have advised that you should be consulted.

The letter was dated from Washington and bore the sig-
nature of Edward D. Bates, Attorney General of the United
States.

Well, he had come to the right man. Jim Eads was
known to every riverman from the Falls of St. Anthony to
the Head of Passes, and most of them knew him personally; one of those characters so readily thrown off by the
second generation of pioneering stock, with a vivid drive
toward building, doing things better. When their skills
were insufficient, they learned new ones and when their
tools were inadequate they invented better ones.

Jim Eads began as an apple-boy, which means that he
sold apples along the decks of river ships and listened to

the outrageous tales of the rivermen, almost half of them true, since nothing was impossible in that age and place. He grew up tall, strong, and so good a chess player that he could handle several simultaneous games blindfolded. The river steamers had to be frail for light draft and speed; before he was 18 Jim Eads became exercised over the number that tore their bottoms out on snags or capsized after hitting bars. He invented a diving bell, which was only a kind of barrel turned upside down, for the recovery of lost goods. A "mechanic" refused to have anything to do with the contraption; Eads went down in it himself and raped a wreck of so much of her valuable cargo that it gave him ideas.

His education had been limited to what he could pick up haphazard, but now he designed a mechanically proper diving bell and a ship with a catamaran hull that could straddle a sunken wreck, and took the designs to Case & Nelson, shipbuilders. They built bell and boat on shares. Eads called the ship *Submarine,* did most of his own diving, and made money hand over fist, in view of the fact that whatever he fished up was property abandoned under water and belonged to him alone. About this time he fell in love with a girl who married him over parental objections but insisted that rivermen were a bunch of crude scoundrels; so he sold *Submarine* and invested the proceeds in a glass factory. It failed, leaving him $35,000 in the hole. He went back to the river, where he had no difficulty in having two new *Submarines,* of improved design, built on credit.

This was in 1851; there were more wrecks than ever and fatter pickings. By the time Eads got to *Submarine No. 7,* she was a giant that could raise a ship's hull entire, and had huge centrifugal pumps for clearing sand and water from the wreck. By 1857 he was operating ten salvage vessels and had become one of the wealthiest men in the west, but his wife died of cholera aboard an Ohio River boat before he could get her to a doctor, and he had so sought surcease in violent labor that the medical men told him he must rest completely. There was a second marriage—to a cousin's widow and apparently more for companionship than love—and at 37 he retired to read and think.

One of the things he thought about was the reports from the war in the Crimea, where certain French floating batteries plated with iron had bombarded the Russian shore forts without receiving the slightest damage. When the Southern states seceded, it was clear as diamond to Jim Eads that the Confederates would bar the great river with forts. He set to work on the design of a river-going modification of the French iron batteries, something to batter these forts without being battered in return. Soon after Lincoln's inauguration he wrote a letter about this idea to Edward Bates, the grandfatherly Missouri lawyer and politician who so nearly missed the Republican nomination, and whom, of course, he knew well. First result: the letter perceived in Act I, Scene 1. Second result: a telegram a few days later: *Come to Washington.*

There was a Cabinet conference on the matter, Bates and the Blairs having so much influence that it was advisable to give a full hearing to anything they backed. As Eads developed his scheme, it was to begin with *Submarine No. 7*, whose powerful engines would enable her to carry guns and armor, once the weight of special salvage equipment had been removed. The rebel forts would naturally be placed at bends in the rivers; therefore end-on fire would be all that was needed and only the prow need carry armor. Piled cotton bales would protect the sides.

Eads had sketches. Lincoln's opinion is not recorded, but
all the Cabinet were in favor except Simon Cameron of
War, who ridiculed the whole idea.

Mr. Navy Secretary Welles thought enough of the plan
to ask Eads to explain it to a board of officers, which was
done the next day. They approved and the sketches were
passed to Samuel M. Pook, naval constructor, to be trans-
lated into plans in accordance with naval practice. This
Pook had been designing warships, mostly for sail, since
1835, and had a great reputation within the service, but
kept himself much in the background and rarely spoke
unless he was addressed.

At this point the proceedings were interrupted by a
See Here! from Simon Cameron. Navy, he said, had no
authority to do anything on the rivers; they were exclu-
sively under army jurisdiction. He carried his point in the
Cabinet; Pook had to send Eads' sketches back to him; and
Eads had to sit around his hotel, waiting for answers to
his letters to Cameron. They never came, since the War
Secretary was deep in his usual habit of keeping his files
in his pocket and answering nothing that did not promise
some immediate gain. After several days of waiting, Eads
wrote a letter to Welles, setting forth in ink what he had
said verbally about river gunboats, then went back to St.
Louis to tell his troubles to Frank Blair.

He arrived on May 11, just in time to be present when
the swine from the German gutters and their redheaded
captain made prisoners of the knights of Camp Jackson,
and to see the street fighting that followed. This local
Union triumph was quite correctly attributed to Blair's
work in the background, and Blair credit stood high when
Eads returned to Washington with the politician's blessing. Cameron was prodded into action; he asked that a

naval officer be detailed to consult with Mr. Eads and General McClellan (of the Department of Ohio) on the best means of establishing a "naval armament" on the river to blockade commercial traffic with the seceded states.

Welles gave him Commander John Rodgers, son of the old 1812 commodore, a sufficiently strange choice, since Rodgers had been on the North Pacific Hydrographic Survey for almost ten years, knew very little about steam and almost nothing about the rivers. In view of the hyperbolic increase in the demand for officers to make good the Atlantic blockade, there was probably no one better available; anyway Welles backed up Rodgers by sending Pook out a week or so later to survey ships.

Meanwhile Rodgers had reached St. Louis, instantly rejected the project of turning *Submarine No. 7* into an armorclad as fantastic and pushed on to Cincinnati. There he saw General McClellan, who thought it would be well to purchase ships that would be useful on smaller rivers as well as on the Mississippi. Rodgers was a man who Got Things Done, being not too particular about the details, and his first step, claiming jurisdiction over all shipping on western waters, transports included, did not endear him to the army men. The next was to meet Pook in Cincinnati early in June and, after inspection, to buy three side-wheel river steamers, *Lexington, Tyler,* and *Conestoga.*

Under plans drawn on the spot by Pook, the tall cabins were cut down to a single deck, the sides plated with five inches of oak plank, "which I found by experiment is a sufficient guard against small arms," and the decks braced for guns. The ships would be ready on June 27. Rodgers sent requisitions for navy men for crews and 16 32-pounders for armament.

He got neither. Welles told him sharply that since river

operations were under the War Department, requisitions must be addressed to that office, that he must enlist rivermen for crews, and that he had no authority to buy or alter boats except by army orders. Rodgers eventually cleared up the last by getting McClellan to approve his purchases, and somehow straightened out the bookkeeping so that an assortment of guns was shipped to him, mostly from the Lake Erie station. The result was patchwork armaments in all three—*Conestoga*, 4 32-pounders and a light piece; *Lexington*, 4 8-inch, 2 32-pounders; *Tyler*, 6 8-inch, 1 32-pounder; and each ship having one gun arranged to fire astern. The three did not get to army headquarters at Cairo, Illinois, until August, with *Conestoga* leaking badly and all more or less battered after having gone aground again and again.

Eads thought all three were monstrosities and pointed out this was exactly what he had predicted. Lieutenant S. Ledyard Phelps thought *Conestoga* had been built by "Irish immigrants instead of mechanics"; there were no passing boxes for the ammunition and the magazines were dreadfully vulnerable. Rodgers had managed to get some young naval lieutenants to command the gunboats and to enroll some rivermen who would "make good artillerists with training," but was still horribly short of crews and could only get a promise of 1000 Atlantic fishermen at some future date. He was unable even to make his "more auspicious" name of *Taylor* stick to *Tyler* (ex-President Tyler of Virginia having Gone with His State). In fact, the naval commander quarreled with everybody about this war not being run according to regulations, and about the time the gunboats reached Cairo asked to be sent to the coast; at the same time the military requested his relief. He was a man born for trouble.

## II

Meanwhile Eads, though so unceremoniously ejected from the picture by Rodgers, was by no means through. Pook returned to Washington from his western trip filled with enthusiasm, if not for Eads' sketches, at least for Eads' idea; and the Blair interests supplying the push as before, he was commissioned to design a gunboat. He drew plans for a 512-ton vessel, 175 feet long and 50 feet in beam, with a draft of six feet. There was to be no keel in the ordinary sense—only a kind of dividing cutwater under the prow before the bottom became completely flat. Atop this hull an oblong casemate sloped up to a flat roof, 45 degrees in front, 35 on the side; its forward end was to hold 3 9- or 10-inch guns; there were to be 4 32-pounders on each beam and lighter guns astern. In front she was protected by $2\frac{1}{2}$ inches of iron, and the same amount covered the engines and paddle-wheels, set amidships aft; the rest was heavy planking as in the Rodgers gunboats. Atop was a conical pilothouse, lightly plated with iron. Nobody had ever seen or imagined such a ship before; it was a work of the purest imagination, like Jules Verne's cannon to fire to the moon, with only the inspiration coming from the Eads sketches.

Experience would show that it was not a perfect piece of design. The ships were miserably slow; the guns were only a couple of feet above water; and the portholes were too big except in the one direction where it was important they should be big, that is, above, for elevating the pieces. The furnaces were so close to the deck that it had to be sanded and wetted to keep from catching fire when full speed was called for. The armor on the pilothouse was far from adequate and that on the casemate not very; on the upper deck there was no armor at all; only water-level combat was envisaged. But at the time, with the materials and knowledge available, and under the burning urgency of a war, it was a far-from-discreditable performance on the part of old Sam Pook.

Also, it was probably just as well that it went through Army instead of Navy. John Lenthall, the Chief Naval Constructor, thought the whole project inpracticable; but General Joseph Totten of Army Ordnance, who knew nothing about ships but what he had learned by shooting at them, advertised for bids on seven of these ungainly craft. Of course Jim Eads was low bidder, at $89,600 each, with a proviso to complete the seven in 65 days from contract, signed August 7.

Men were out of jobs. It had not yet become clear that the economic impact of the war would be to raise to major importance the transfer of western wheat by railroad to the North Atlantic seaports for shipment to Europe. The visible facts were that the wheat could no longer be shipped by barge and steamer through New Orleans, that no longer did the machine shops of Pittsburgh receive orders for machinery from Natchez, or the lumber mills of Wisconsin get requests for dressed timber to build new houses in Memphis. It was easier to go for a three months' man than to see the wife begging credit from the grocer under such conditions.

Into this situation leaped Jim Eads, with a reputation for always paying largely and a demand for people who would take a job that combined profit and patriotism. He knew the potential employers of labor and reached them all via the telegraph lines; they all knew him and the soundness of his checks. Within two weeks he had 4000 men at work, from machine shops in Pennsylvania to mines in Wisconsin and sawmills in Michigan, and the "keels" of four ironclads were laid at the Carondelet of St. Louis.

On September 6 there arrived before Eads a certain Captain Andrew H. Foote, USN, with the temporary rank of Flag Officer Commanding the Mississippi Squadron (Army). He was a small man with a rough beard around an aggressive chin; had been a classmate of Gideon Welles back in the Cheshire Academy, where he agreed with the now Secretary of the Navy that Rome should have suffered the fate of Carthage rather than her language be studied by young Americans. Foote had developed into a genuine hellfire Presbyterian, who could preach a dandy sermon, and did on numerous occasions. He had been much in the Far East and fought the barbarous Malays there; Welles sent him to the river command because, beside being a man he had known since schooldays, his capacity in dealing with savages might make him useful in handling the army.

Foote's first reaction to the Pook gunboats was utterly unfavorable, but the young officers who came out with him to command the ships were so enthusiastic that he allowed himself a qualified degree of conversion. From this time forth he addressed a series of urgent demands to Washington for men and equipment, and meanwhile set up a naval base at Mound City, up the Ohio from Cairo. It was one of the strangest ever seen, everything afloat—wharf-boats, tugs, barges, and old steamers linked together, with machine shops aboard using newly made machine tools that had been floated down the river from Pittsburgh. They were employed to make engines for the three gunboats laid down in addition to the four at the

Carondelet. Eads gladly furnished some of his mechanics; there was not room for them all to work at his base.

On October 12, *St. Louis* floated out, the first of the ironclads; but now came a series of vexatious eruptions and interruptions. By the end of the month Eads had used up all his personal bank credit without receiving a cent from Washington, where the inefficient Cameron was still keeping his office in his pockets. The builder told Foote that work would have to stop, whereupon the latter's expression "became demoniac" to such a degree that Eads borrowed money from all his friends to meet the payrolls. The Fourth Auditor decided that service on the river was not sea service, and refused to allow the sailors more than retired pay, for which they refused to serve. Eads went to Washington and came back depressed; Quartermaster General Montgomery Meigs wanted a forfeit of $10,000 on each ship, because it was taking nearer a hundred days to finish them than the contract 65. He was unwilling to listen to pleas that the delay had been caused by shortage of money, the laying aside of Eads' work by the Pittsburgh iron foundries to make ordnance for the army, and changes introduced into the design by Pook as things went along.

More favorable was the arrival at St. Louis of General John Charles Frémont, all soul and glory, the "Pathfinder of the West," husband of old Senator Benton's daughter, and ex-candidate for President. He came late in July, just before the redheaded captain, now General Nathaniel Lyon, got himself killed at Wilson's Creek in a battle that was a technical defeat for the Union but lamed the Confederacy in that quarter for nearly a year. John Charles Frémont was a lot of noise and so little efficient that he failed to last out '61; but he was a charter member of the Blair Gang, and since Eads was associated with that gang when he took his projects to Frémont, they were promptly approved by the high command.

One of these ideas was for the employment of *Submarine No. 7* on the original Eads design, heavily modified by Pook.[1] Her bottom was carried across from one hull to the other, she was decked over amidships in the same manner, and bottom and deck carried forward to make a stubby prow. Instead of the two outside wheels she received a single one amidships; the regular Pook casemate was installed, but in view of the ship's size (200 by 75 feet) and engine power, was given $3\frac{1}{2}$-inch plates all along, except at the stern. They named her *Benton* and armed her with 2 9-inch, 7 army 42-pound rifles, and 7 32-pounders, the most powerful ship in the fleet and also the slowest. Captain John Ancrum Winslow was her commander; when she got aground on the way to Cairo, with ice already floating down the river, hawsers were led ashore and through a chain to a ringbolt in the side of the ship. As the steam was applied, the chain broke and a big piece of it went halfway through Winslow's arm. He had to be invalided home.

Another Eads-Frémont alteration was *Essex,* a river ferryboat cut down, bigger than the Pook ships, not as big as *Benton,* with slightly lighter plating than the latter, armed with 3 9-inch, 1 10-inch, and 2 32-pounders; Foote liked her as a flagship because she was so commodious below.

---

[1] Frémont had no authority to approve anything of the kind, but he was a man who seldom worried about the legality of what he did. Quartermaster General Meigs was suspicious of the deal because Eads owned the ship; the only thing really phony about it was that he sold her to the army for a third of her value.

The squadron over which he hoisted his flag on January 11, 1862, with ice bumping the gunwales and all the ships far short of their complements, thus comprised *Lexington* (Commander R. N. Stembel, later Lieutenant J. L. Shirk), *Tyler* (Commander Henry Walke, later Lieutenant-Commander William Gwin), *Conestoga* (Lieutenant S. Ledyard Phelps), all these being wooden gunboats; *Benton* (Lieutenant George M. Blodgett), *Essex* (Lieutenant W. D. "Dirty Bill" Porter); with the seven that speedily became known as the "Pook turtles"; *St. Louis* (Lieutenant Commander Leonard Paulding), *Cairo* (Lieutenant Thomas O. Selfridge, Jr.), *Carondelet* (Walke), *Cincinnati* (Stembel), *Louisville* (Commander B. M. Dove), *Pittsburg*[2] (Lieutenant Commander E. Thompson), *Mound City* ( Commander A. H. Kilty). All the skippers were young lieutenants; and despite the terrible labor pains in bringing it to birth, it was the largest fleet yet assembled under the American flag.

### III

Before ice and low water made river operations unappetizing, the wooden gunboats had begun the war. The command of the military district of southeast Missouri had been given to one U. S. Grant, a retired army captain, reclaimed and made brigadier, in charge of as much of Kentucky and Tennessee as he could take. Paducah he quickly seized and garrisoned, but not before Confederate General (and Bishop) Leonidas Polk decided to make Chickasaw Bluff[3] at Columbus into a great place of arms

2 The name of the city was often and that of the ship always spelled without the H.

3 There are several sets of Chickasaw Bluffs in this story; the Chickasaw were a people who got around, and almost everywhere some headland was named after them.

which would hold the river secure against the Union. At the foot of these bluffs he established a floating battery of 16 guns; 50 feet up were two rifled pieces, and on the crest of the bluffs themselves, 350 feet above the stream, a series of big pivoted guns, arranged for plunging fire. An English correspondent who saw them at practice thought he "would rather be near the target than the battery."

General Grant, in the intervals of training his raw troops at the Cairo base, developed an intense curiosity about this installation and, almost as soon as Foote arrived, asked him to take an armed ship down the river for a demonstration. Foote gave him *Tyler* and Henry Walke; the ship took aboard 100 men from the 9th Illinois in case of accident and ran 20 miles downstream. Of course Polk's guns all began yapping as soon as *Tyler* appeared, satisfactorily revealing their number and position to General Grant. Their practice was not good and Walke made it worse by moving in slow, irregular circles as he fired back. The hits he made on the batteries and the damage he did there (as reported by that most unreliable reporter, the "intelligent contraband" Negro) were a hint that the old doctrine of the helplessness of ships against forts might no longer be valid if the guns were big enough. On the way back to Cairo there was another hint; the banks were lined with Confederate riflemen and anyone who stuck his head above the bulwarks got a hole through it.

This brings the story to November when Frémont, who had done nothing but hold vainglorious levees and enlist a bodyguard of hussars in Hungarian uniforms, gave signs of taking the field against the rebels in southwest Missouri. Grant was desired to do something to pin General Polk's forces in the Columbus fortress to keep them from rein-

forcing the enemy across the river. Direct attack on Columbus, either overland or by water, was beyond his resources,
but he conceived that the enemy might feel menaced by
a crack at their fortified camp of Belmont, on the low-
lying Missouri shore, a little above Columbus. The reconnaissance of the latter place had given him a much higher
idea of the gunboats than he held previously; he asked for
naval support, and Foote assigned *Tyler,* under Walke's
command, with *Lexington* and Stembel.

Before dawn of the morning of November 16 the expedition set out, with all the transports Grant had carrying
an Iowa regiment and four from Illinois, 3100 men all
told. The gunboats moved down and took on the Columbus batteries, while Grant's men landed in a cornfield.
Walke circled again; it is probable that his guns did not
much more damage than the forts did to him, until after
some three hours a shot came through the side and penetrated the deck to kill one man. Almost simultaneously
Walke noticed that the firing in the direction of Belmont
had ceased, an "ominous circumstance." It was reported
that farther downstream, out of range of the ships' guns,
several steamers had crossed to deposit some thousands of
rebels on the Missouri shore.

The naval commander turned back, therefore, and
brought his ships to the landing just in time to see about
7000 Confederates advancing in nice even lines to cut
Grant's force from the transports toward which the men
were struggling. The lines were beautifully perpendicular
to the broadsides of the ships and not 50 yards away.
Walke opened with shell from the 8-inch; the lines lost
their nicety and presently disappeared back into the woods
from which they had come. The Confederate artillery
tried to reply, but they had only 6-pounders, which lasted

very badly under the impact of the 64-pounders from the big guns of the ships.

Thus Grant and his men got out safely and Walke went back with his gunboat to bring out a party that had remained behind to collect wounded. The Battle of Belmont became a naval victory over land forces, the first of the war in the West, and it was demonstrated that heavy guns could be moved faster on water than on land.

# 2

# The Rebel Reply

An act of the Confederate Congress, assembled at Montgomery, Alabama, February 21, 1861, established a Navy Department, and President Davis promptly appointed as Secretary the Honorable Stephen R. Mallory, ex-U.S. Senator from Florida and head of the Senate Naval Committee. He was a kindly man, of strong emotional feelings, earnest, assiduous, and ignorant, who always wore tight pants; by persuasion a Catholic, by education a lawyer, by profession a local politician. He came from Key West and developed an interest in the maritime service chiefly because his home town was a naval station of sorts, and a senator has to specialize in something.

The reasons for the appointment were very greatly geographical, Florida being the fourth state to secede and Mallory's the fourth rank in the Cabinet. His chief need was a navy. He had something less than a proportionate

number of the officers furnished by the Southern states to
the old service, a tremendous haul of over 500 heavy guns
taken at Norfolk Navy Yard when Virginia went out of
the Union, and absolutely nothing else.

The over-all strategy for the rivers, chiefly developed
by Mr. President Jefferson Davis, who so much prided
himself on his West Point diploma, was one of barrier
fortifications, to be supported by mobile elements on both
land and water. Mr. Davis thought of a line of defense
stretching across Missouri and Kentucky, which were or at
least ought to be, Confederate states. The main line of
resistance would be anchored on Columbus, Kentucky,
northernmost point where the bluffs are high enough to
dominate the stream. These bluffs are everywhere on the
eastern bank, which should have been of strategic signifi-
cance, but there is no evidence that Mr. Davis made it so.
From Columbus the line ran to the point where the Tennessee and Cumberland rivers most nearly approach each
other, with Bowling Green as a land salient forward; now
to Mill Spring at the eastern end, to cover Cumberland
Gap, the line of the Cumberland River being generally
followed. It was a book concept, but one generally correct
by the books of the period; rail and road transport were
insignificant beside that on the great rivers, which made
effective seacoasts of their banks. Any force that jutted in
between the strongpoints would have poor logistic support
and would be exposed to destructive flanking counter-
attack.

General Leonidas Polk of "Department 2," comprising
Mississippi and western Tennessee, therefore moved forward with an "Army of Liberation," 15,000 strong, on
September 4, 1861, seized and began to fortify the bluffs
at Columbus, while General Simon B. Buckner was sent

to Bowling Green and the editor-made-general Felix K. Zollicoffer established himself at Mill Spring.

Forts were built on the Cumberland and Tennessee. Behind this line Vicksburg on the middle Mississippi, where dominating bluffs command the water, was an obvious place for fortifications, and they were built. The situation in Missouri had become very fluid and there was no good point to fortify, but on the Mississippi, 60 miles below Columbus, at the Tennessee-Kentucky line, the river swings a perfect S-curve around Island No. 10, right north to New Madrid before turning south again. The Tennessee side of the river is high ground in a semicircle around the run past the Island; from the Island itself a long stretch up the river could be commanded. On island and opposing bluffs General Polk directed the erection of a complex of 11 forts, mounting a total of not less than 60 guns, mostly 24- and 32-pounders, but some heavy.[1] To these was added a 16-gun battery on the water, ingeniously fashioned from a floating dry dock towed up from New Orleans to the upper end of the Island. Its main feature was its pumps, which made it possible to lower the whole structure till only the iron-plated slanting sides were above water.

Lesser works, Fort Pillow, Fort Randolph, Fort Harris, were established on the bluffs between Island No. 10 and Memphis, as a cover for that city and to keep the Federals from crossing the Missouri below Columbus. There were difficulties about transporting guns from the east, and only Fort Pillow became important; by April of '62 it had 40 guns.

[1] The surviving Confederate records are vague on the number and position of the guns and when the Yankees later took the place, they reported only in general terms. There was some alteration during the progress of events.

All these upriver plans except the building of the forts turned out badly. Kentucky had proclaimed her neutrality in this struggle; the advance of Polk, Buckner, and Zollicoffer therefore constituted an invasion that brought the state fully to the side of the Union. Buckner found there were too many abolitionists around for him to maintain his Bowling Green salient without river support, and had to fall back to the Cumberland; while Zollicoffer was injudicious enough to attack a force under General George H. Thomas in January of 1862. Thomas gave the first sign of what he was to become; Zollicoffer was killed, his force broken up, and the strategic situation in eastern Kentucky became dubious. Confederate troops were attracted to the area and the strategy of combined arms was affected, since the men had to be taken from Henry and Donelson, the forts on the Tennessee and Cumberland.

On the Tennessee, indeed, the building of the works themselves was affected. It was planned as a double fortress, Henry on the right bank, a bastioned pentagon covering a long, straight stretch of stream from low level, with a heavy rifled Parrott, an 8-inch Columbiad, 2 42-pound rifles, 16 32-pounders; 12 of them, including all the big pieces, bore downstream. Fort Heiman on the bluffs across, but a step inland, dominated Henry but not the stream. As a result of the Mill Spring defeat and the switch-over of men, Heiman never did get completed, nor did the elaborate system of lines which was to connect Henry with Donelson.

Donelson was an altogether more formidable work than Henry. The land side ran a mile between two creeks, between which a high hill heaved up to descend in bluffs to the banks of the Cumberland, 120 feet tall at its topmost point, where guns were mounted for plunging fire, with another battery at the 50-foot level and a third at 20 feet. All told it had 8 32-pounders, 2 32-pound carronades, 2 9-inch, 1 10-inch Columbiad, and 1 10-inch 128-pound rifle—fewer guns than Henry but heavier and better placed.

Columbus was more powerful than either, but events made the details of its armament unimportant. Island No. 10, Vicksburg, and Port Hudson below the latter were still receiving their artillery at this point.

## II

The forts at the mouth of the Mississippi were Jackson and St. Philip, star-shaped masonry works facing each other at a bend in the stream, some 15 miles above the point where the river spreads into its delta, some 75 miles from the city. They were part of the permanent defenses of the United States, cleaned up and strengthened by the Confederates when they took over. Jackson had 24 of its 74 guns in casemates, which means they had overhead and lateral as well as front protection; the woods were cut away along the bank to give a long arc of fire before the fort could be reached by a ship coming up. St. Philip fired directly downstream and had 52 guns. The main feature of the combination was that any ship coming up would have to slow for a sharp right-angled turn under the artillery, just where the current runs swiftest.[2]

---

[2] For the record and reference, Jackson had in its water battery, newly mounted: a 10-inch Columbiad, 2 8-inch Columbiads, a 10-inch mortar, 2 32-pound rifles. In the casemates: 10 24-pound howitzers, 1 8-inch howitzer, 14 24-pound guns. In the barbettes above: 2 10-inch Columbiads, 3 8-inch Columbiads, 1 7-inch rifle, 2 8-inch howitzers, 6 42-pound rifles, 15 32-pounders, 11 24-pounders, 1 7⅜-inch howitzer. And on the parade: a 6-pounder and a 12-pound howitzer. St. Philip was armed with 4 8-inch Columbiads, 1 24-pounder, 1 13-inch mortar, 1 10-inch mortar, 1 8-inch mortar, 16 24-pounders, all these being above; in the water battery were

Between the forts was built an obstruction of heavy cypress logs, 40 to 60 feet long, four to five feet thick, held together with chains and to the bottom by 30 anchors. It lasted three months before being carried away by winter high water, after which it was replaced by another boom of small vessels chained together. Between them the two cost $100,000, and there were those, especially among naval men, who did not think the money well spent.

These fixed defenses, of course, were all strictly Confederate States Army enterprises. The navy's part in river defense was earliest in the hands of Captain Lawrence Rousseau of Louisiana, senior officer on the list of those who went South, and a man whom some of the Dixie newspapers wanted for Navy Secretary instead of Mallory. He was in his sixties and not active; in July of '61 Mallory called him to Richmond, to use his knowledge of men and their records in the Bureau of Orders and Detail—both the personnel and logistic support department of the Confederate Navy. He was replaced in the river command by Commodore George N. Hollins.

This Hollins had been a mid in the War of 1812 and served under Decatur; he was a Southern-thinking Marylander who resigned the service in June, was commissioned by the Confederacy, and instantly organized a hasty raid on the lower reaches of the Potomac. It captured a steamer loaded with coal, another with coffee, and a third with a load of ice. This marked him; Mallory, who believed heartily in the 1812 tradition that an overwhelming naval opponent could be beaten to her knees, sent him to New

9 32-pounders, 6 42-pounders, 1 7-inch rifle, 1 8-inch Columbiad, 4 24-pounders; with 4 10-inch mortars in a field work, and 1 6-, 1 12-, and 1 24-pound howitzer on the parade. It was a wild assemblage of armament, anything that could be found, and must have made ammunition supply difficult. Both forts were extensively reinforced with courses of sandbags.

Orleans as a dashing operational officer, probably without realizing that the first requirement of dashing operations is something to operate with.

Hollins took command on the last day of July, finding on hand an authorization from Mallory to Rousseau to take into government service whatever vessels Governor Moore of Louisiana deemed proper. Governor Moore had apparently not deemed very much proper. Hollins had to use Navy Department funds for the purchase of several river steamers, which before the end of the year became *Stonewall Jackson* (ex-*Yankee*), *Ivy*, *General Polk*, and *Tuscarora*. In January and February of 1862 he added *Ponchartrain* (ex-*Lizzie Simmons*), *Webb*, *Calhoun*, and *Maurepas* (ex-*Grostète*). They were of tonnage most various and most of their records are now gone, but the general picture was that they were low-sided river towboats, not the floating castles Mark Twain used to pilot. The bows of all were strengthened with iron for ramming; all received at least a 32-pounder smoothbore forward and a lighter rifled gun aft, with such other artillery as their decks could stand. Better than any of this lot was *McRae* (ex-*Marques de la Habana*), an oceangoing screw-propeller ship armed with a 9-inch and 6 32-pounders, which had been intended as an ocean raider but was found too slow for that duty.

In addition there was an orphan craft named *Manassas*, constructed and probably designed by J. O. Curtis as a privateer at the behest of a syndicate of merchants soon after the Confederate Congress passed its privateering act in May. The basis was a powerful tug, *Enoch Train*, built in Boston six years before. Curtis strengthened her longitudinally with 17-inch beams and gave her an iron ram bow; then covered her with a turtleback right down to the water on all sides, making her look like a sharp-pointed egg. Her carapace was 12-inch oak, covered with 1½-inch iron; in the bow a 68-pounder was mounted, with a shutter that closed automatically when the gun was retracted for loading. The only entrance was through a hatch in her back and the only ventilation came through this and the gunport, so she must have been somewhat stuffy. When completed, she had a speed of about four knots, altogether too slow for a privateer on the high seas, so the state bought her and forward-passed her to Hollins.

### III

But all this was only part of a temporary emergency program; Mallory's heart was really set on the development of an ironclad fleet that should be strong enough to put the whole Federal navy at defiance. A central fact in this pattern of thinking was that he knew enough of naval history to realize that the genuinely glorious victories won against the Royal Navy in 1812 had been gained by ships that were generally stronger and better gunned than their opponents; but he did not know enough to be aware that the essential feature of those victories was the skill of the American captains and the wonderful precision training of their crews. In the mind of the former head of the Senate Naval Committee (which was mainly concerned with ship construction) the ship was all; and he was powerfully encouraged in this attitude by his chief of the Bureau of Ordnance and Hydrography, John M. Brooke, and his Chief Naval Constructor, John L. Porter.

Brooke, "a very dark looking man who did not impress a stranger with being as great a genius as he really was," had invented the Brooke rifle, the ancestor of modern naval guns.[3] Both he and Porter had conducted firing tests against inclined wooden targets faced with iron. Both were convinced that the only way of breaking the blockade proclaimed by Lincoln in April was ironclads, and they convinced Mallory; as early as May 8 the Secretary was asking Congress for them.

There has been considerable argument as to whether Brooke or Porter was chiefly responsible for what became the standard Confederate type ironclad, with the sloping casemate and the sharp ends below water. The fact seems to be that at the time the two men collaborated without jealousy or question. One thing not realized either by them or by Mallory was the time factor of which Jim Eads was so thoroughly cognizant. The Confederates had agents among Eads' workers, and Mallory knew all about the ironclad menace from the upper river, but it was August 24 before the Confederate Congress passed an act for the construction of two ironclad rams by John T. Shirley of Memphis.

Named *Arkansas* and *Tennessee,* they were of the normal Brooke-Porter type, like the famous *Virginia* (ex-*Merrimack*), but built from the keel up instead of being alterations; twin-propeller ships with one engine to each propeller, yielding a speed of six knots against the water; 165 feet long, 35 feet in beam and 11½ in draft; armed with 2 8-inch Columbiads ahead, 1 9-inch Dahlgren, 2 32-pounders, and a 6-inch rifle on each beam and 2 6-inch rifles astern; a crew of 200 men.

---

3 The inner tube of the gun was cast; then wrought-iron bands of slightly less interior circumference were heated until they expanded enough to fit over the core and the whole allowed to cool. This gives a gun of great strength against the internal explosion without excessive total weight.

Shirley's contract called for the completion of both ships by December 24, but he began by finding out that he had to build sawmills before he could cut timber and then that he had to buy iron for the armor in 50- and 100-pound lots from all over the South. Ship carpenters were sought for in New Orleans, Mobile, and Nashville; the word was that they had volunteered or been conscripted into the army. In spite of a personal appeal from Secretary Mallory, General Polk flatly refused to release a man. The work on the twin ironclads therefore dragged around the turn of the year and into the time when actual operations began.

Near New Orleans, the only other river port which possessed viable shipyards, Hollins began construction on three wooden gunboats, *Livingston, Bienville,* and *Carondelet,* which were never finished and are only mentioned to complete the roster. He also contracted with the firm of E. C. Murray for the ironclad ram *Louisiana.* This was a formidable and highly original ship, outwardly of the usual Brooke-Porter casemate-and-submerged-ends type, but with important internal differences, due to the availability of materials and Murray's experience in river design. Thus the armor consisted of T-shaped rails set vertically, the inner courses bolted to the wooden structure, the outer ones reversed and driven down the gaps. Propulsion was by a pair of wheels set tandem amidships, and steering with a tiller, helped by two small propellers set at the corners of the nearly square stern. She was armed with 16 guns: 2 9-inch and a 7-inch rifle ahead, 2 8-inch and 1 7-inch rifle astern, 2 8-inch and 3 32-pound rifles starboard, 1 9-inch and 4 32-pound rifles port, a more powerful armament than *Virginia.*

The shortage of raw materials experienced up the river

was a drawback here also, and the ram was not laid down until October 15, at which date the first of Eads' ships was already launched. In addition there were labor troubles caused by lack of money. The Confederate Congress appropriated and Mallory duly requisitioned Treasury; but Treasury Secretary C. G. Memminger only sent Confederate bonds to New Orleans, and neither banks nor laborers would have such stuff. The men went on strike for four or five days at a stretch, once for four weeks, while the indigestible bonds were returned to Richmond and exchanged for Treasury notes, which were accepted, but with some suspicion. There was no shop to build engines at New Orleans, so the ram's power plant was taken from the fast river steamer *Ingomar*; it took two months to dismantle the ship and move the engines to *Louisiana*. In February, when fighting started in the north, the ironclad was a long way from completion, and Governor Moore had just telegraphed Richmond that the Navy Department owed nearly a million and its credit was stopped.

Most important of all was the second New Orleans ironclad, *Mississippi*. She grew out of the brains of two brothers named Tift, Nelson and Asa, residents of Georgia and Florida for 30 years, and so sincere Confederate patriots that Asa had been a member of his state's secession convention. But they were natives of Connecticut, which paved their way with suspicion, and later when things went wrong, they were arrested as damyankee spies.

At the start, however, it was all honey and roses. The Tifts were not naval designers or engineers, but rich merchants, and early in the new administration they turned up in Richmond with a model for a new type of ship. Brooke, Porter, and a detail of engineers in Mallory's department made some changes, so no one can say precisely what the original model was. But as *Mississippi* reached launching point she came out a vessel of over 4000 tons, 270 feet long, 58 feet in beam, with a 14-foot draft, a strong casemate of two feet of oak covered by three inches of iron, an iron ram bow over a casing three feet thick, 20 casemate guns, and above them a "shooting gallery" where sharp-shooters were to be occupied in picking off enemy officers.

The most original feature of this monster (aside from her size) were her engine plant and the manner of her building. The former comprised three engines of 36-inch bore and 30-inch stroke, driving as many shafts, which were supposed to yield the ship horsepower enough for 14 knots, or more than any warship in the world had ever done. The building was arranged on a complete system of angled beams, so that ordinary house carpenters instead of those experienced on ship construction could put her to-gether. The Tifts asked nothing for her but their traveling expenses, rigidly audited.

With his predilection for the invincible warship, Mallory was enthusiastic from the first; Brooke and Porter were part of a board that reported on her with extreme favor. The Secretary appointed the two Tifts navy agents and sent them to New Orleans, where they closed with E. C. Murray to build their craft in a newly prepared ship-yard north of the city. Half a dozen different ship designers and engineers puzzled over the problem of working out the details at the level of practical construction; it was September 28 before E. M. Ivens and Chief Engineer Warner had produced drawings that would satisfy both the Tifts and the demands of marine stability, and work could actually begin.

The troubles began with the work. The Tifts had no contract to impose financial limits and could pay anything they wished for materials and labor—that is, they worked on a cost-plus basis, which endeared them to the house carpenters and suppliers of material. This resulted in the woodwork being completed 110 days from the time when the ship was begun, in spite of the fact that the army took some of the best workmen and had to be squeezed to let them go.

But the people who were to build engines and shafts were already working for the government on jobs that had priority—locomotives, for example—and could not see why they should change over their whole shop equipment and procedure for a one-shot operation. Add to this a certain amount of unpopularity the Tifts earned with their dam-yankee notions about high-speed work for high pay in an essentially leisurely and conservative society. They were vigorously supported by Commodore Hollins, but it was December before the Patterson Iron Works would undertake to build the main engine.

Even more difficult was the problem of shafting. The three had to be nine inches in diameter, the two outer ones 40 feet long, the center shaft 50 feet, and all of wrought iron, not the usual cast iron of river-vessel shafting because of the strains. There was not a foundry or a hammer in the Confederacy that could make them. Patterson Iron finally agreed to remodel their equipment to make the outer shafts, but then had to wait for an experienced hammer man from Richmond, and the year had turned before work started. The center shaft was utterly beyond Patterson's capacity; the Tredegar Iron Works of Richmond began work on it, but not until February, 1862.

## IV

An old boffer named General Daniel E. Twiggs, second

ranking officer of the U. S. Army, who had served with courage if not discretion in 1812 and Mexico, commanded the Southwest at the time of secession. He surrendered the nine posts he held and became commander of "Department No. 1," most importantly Louisiana. About all he did in office was issue orders for the punishment of those who furnished the "Black Republican ships" with provisions, and being weighted with years he asked to be relieved from active duty in September of 1861.

In his room Davis appointed Major General Mansfield Lovell. This slender, brown-haired man was a sufficiently strange character, a native of Washington city, who went through West Point with credit, served in the Mexican War with spirit enough to win a brevet and a citation, then resigned the service in 1854 to become an executive in an iron works at Trenton. This failed to satisfy; he went to New York, joined the Sons of St. Tammany, and was made street commissioner. Three of his brothers lived in the South and he thought she was perfectly right in this contest, but it was not until August, 1861, a month after Bull Run, that he cut all Northern connections and went to Lexington, Kentucky. As of that date there is a letter from General Joe Johnston to President Davis, recommending Lovell as fit for the command of at least a division, but remarking that as a man who did not come from a seceded state "he did not know how he would be received." Davis was anxious to employ as many able Northerners as he could, which explains the major general's commission and the appointment to New Orleans.

He was to take office on October 7, 1861, and arrived on approximately that date, to find the defense of the city in a state he thought appalling. Nobody seemed interested in improving things; people were invincibly patriotic and went down to Fort Jackson for champagne parties, but nobody piled sandbags and the blockade was already causing a shortage of needles. It was about this same date that Secretary of War Walker, having demonstrated his complete incapacity for any sort of public business, was replaced by Davis' favorite trouble-shooter, Judah P. Benjamin.

Lovell wrote Benjamin, a Louisiana man himself, on October 18, that New Orleans was "greatly drained of arms, ammunition, clothing and supplies for other points." He had no confidence in the forts or the slow process by which the navy was providing for river defense, and the Federal ironclads building upstream were very menacing. This was an annotation on a conversation he had with Benjamin before leaving for New Orleans, in which he laid down that the defense of the city would have to be under a single unified command—his own, of course.

Lovell was asked to prescribe a remedy, and suggested having altered and armed a number of river tow ships, to be commanded by river pilots, manned by rivermen, fitted with what guns they could carry, but principally with strong ram bows that would make them superior in combat to the slow Eads ironclads. On January 12, 1862, Lovell's authorization arrived from Benjamin; he was to impress the steamers *Mexico, Texas, Orizaba, Charles Morgan, Florida, Arizona, Jewess, Atlantic, Houston, Magnolia, Matagorda, Anglo-Saxon,* and *Anglo-Norman.* A river captain named J. E. Montgomery would head the squadron; work was begun on January 16.

The ships, according to Montgomery's own account, had

. . . their machinery protected by an inner bulkhead of 12-inch square timber, bolted together; an outer bulkhead of 6 x 12-inch timber; space between bulkheads 22 inches.

The space between was filled with ordinary size cotton bales, compressed to fit between the bulkheads. The outer bulkheads were plated with railroad iron an inch thick. The bows were made solid with 12-inch-square timber, bolted together and sheathed on the outside with 4-inch oak plank, one by 2½-inch iron was bent around the bow and extended back to the sheathing.

This may be taken as a reasonably good description of the vessels in Hollins' flotilla as well.

Correspondence between the original names and those in the Confederate service is now impossible to establish. The first to be completed were *Warrior* and *Defiance,* March 9; then came *General Bragg* (a seagoing job), *General Price* and *General Van Dorn,* March 25 (the ironwork on the latter two was not completed till April 10 at Memphis); *Resolute* and *Colonel Lovell,* March 31; *General Beauregard,* April 5; *General Jeff Thompson* and *Little Rebel* (another ocean ship with a screw propeller), April 11; *Sumter,* April 17; *General Breckinridge,* April 22. Another *Lovell* of unknown provenance and date, not one of the original lot, crept in sometime during April, *General Lovell.*

The main concern for the defense of the city was those Federal ironclads, already in action by this time, and as fast as the ships were ready, they were sent to Memphis under Montgomery's tactical command, but strategically under Lovell. He grew nervous about an attack from the sea during the proceedings and either recalled or retained *Warrior, Defiance, General Lovell, General Breckinridge,* and *Resolute.* They were called the River Defense Fleet and as completed, each ship had only a 24- and a 32-pounder, but those that reached Memphis received an additional 32-pounder and a number of them an 8-inch apiece.

This made two completely independent fleet commands on the Mississippi and Lovell was by no means satisfied with his, writing as early as January that "fourteen Mississippi river captains and pilots will never agree about anything once they get under way," and bitterly reinforcing his remark from experience in April when the ships were under way:

The river pilots are men of limited ideas, no system and no administrative capacity whatever. Unless some competent person of education, system and business is put over each division of the fleet it will, in my judgement, prove an utter failure. There is little or no discipline or subordination—too much "steamboat" and too little of the "man-of-war" to be very effective.

On top of this Hollins had no authority to supervise work on the ironclads, which were built on orders from Richmond, but Mallory constantly urged him to hurry them along. That is, the roots of confusion were present, and growth was compounded by the fact that the states in their sovereign capacity could not be restrained from having navies of their own. Governor Moore of Louisiana fitted out two of the usual towboats, one named after himself and the other *General Quitman*. Their captains claimed afterward that they were to recognize no authority but that of the Governor and the Secretary of War, and that they had been given papers to this effect. Tennessee got into the act in December, via a telegram from the Governor to Mallory, saying that there were four river steamers at Nashville, suitable for conversion to gunboats, and he wanted to convert them. Mallory sent Lieutenant Isaac M. Brown to make an inspection; the report was favorable on two of the craft, and they were taken in hand for state account, but work never proceeded far on any but *Eastport*.

V

All war is an art of improvisation, but nothing was ever more improvised than the blockade of the Southern ports proclaimed by Lincoln on April 17, 1861. As of that date, the U. S. Navy had exactly ten ships available to cover 3000 miles of coastline, and two of these were needed to keep secure the island forts at Pensacola. It was June before the heavy paddle-wheel sloop *Powhatan* arrived to close the Mississippi mouth at Pas à l'Outre, and the big screw sloop *Brooklyn* that at Southwest Pass. Not long after that Commodore Hollins succeeded in sending to sea the commerce raider *Sumter*, Captain Raphael Semmes, CSN, while *Brooklyn* was chasing a suspicious sail.

*Sumter* at once made her presence so unpleasantly felt on Union merchant ships that Flag Officer W. W. McKean, commanding the Gulf Blockading Squadron, decided there must be a better way of keeping the Mississippi closed than watching the too-numerous exit holes. Geography gave him an opportunity; some 15 miles in there is an area called the Head of Passes, with deep water two miles long and nearly as broad, where all the various passes to the sea branch off at once. By October the Gulf Squadron had been so reinforced by the various marine knicknacks purchased and armed by Mr. Welles that McKean could spare a squadron under Captain "Honest John" Pope for the Head of Passes. It consisted of the heavy screw sloop *Richmond*, with 24 big guns, the sailing sloop *Vincennes*, also with big guns, brig-sloop *Preble* and the little 3-gun side-wheeler *Water Witch,* which was employed chiefly as a towboat for the sailing vessels. This was a not unintelligent distribution of force; the sailing ships were useless in open water against steamers but carried heavy artillery in a quantity far above anything the Confederates could bring against them.

Nevertheless the energetic Hollins had the squadron under observation from the moment of its arrival on October 3, and decided to lay a lance in rest. On October 9 he sent *Ivy* downstream; she had a small-caliber but long-range English Whitworth, which threw shots over *Richmond* without the latter being able to reach her in return, a fact which greatly worried Pope. He wrote off at once for rifled guns of greater range, but before they reached him, Hollins did.

The Confederates came downstream on the night of October 11, with the iron ram *Manassas* leading; behind her marched three fire rafts, flatboats piled with combustible, chained together with a tug on either side of the triplet. The arrangement was that as soon as *Manassas* had struck and presumably crippled *Richmond,* the ram would fire a rocket; whereupon the fire rafts would be ignited and the ships behind close in for gunnery action. These in order were *McRae, Ivy, Tuscarora, Calhoun,* with *Jackson* last, because she had high-pressure engines and the exhaust made such a terrible racket of puffing that it was feared she would give the whole show away.

The night was dark as the inside of a snake, and the tow clumsy, so progress was slow and it was three-forty-five in the morning before the attackers reached the Head of Passes. At this moment *Vincennes* was anchored on the west shore, near the entrance to Southwest Pass, the other three against the east bank, *Preble, Richmond,* and *Water Witch* in that order. There was a coal barge alongside the flagship, from which the deck watch was not very energetically filling her bunkers. It reveals something about Pope that in this age of no searchlights he had not a single picket boat out and the only watches were the anchor watches he would have carried in New York harbor.

The squadron commander's first warning was when a mid burst into his cabin with: "Captain, there's a steamer right alongside of us!" Through a gunport, as he ran for the deck in his nightshirt, Pope saw "an indescribable object" emitting a heavy puff of smoke, and the next moment there was a crash, while the sound of *Preble's* drums boomed through the night, beating to quarters.

As fortune arranged it, *Manassas* struck *Richmond* just where the coal barge was tied to her and, after tearing loose the lashing, crushed three planks in the sloop's side and made a small hole two feet below the waterline. The ram herself was actually more damaged; the shock knocked her engines loose from their mountings and the barge's hawser carried away the funnels flush with the carapace, filling her with smoke, so that she drifted down past *Water Witch,* and it was some time, as time goes in battles, before her crew could separate themselves from their private concerns for long enough to set off their rocket.

The only result of the delay was to afford an opportunity for panic to take a grip on the Union fleet. *Richmond* fired a couple of broadsides at nothing in particular, and through the smoke hoisted three light signals in rapid succession: "ENEMY PRESENT," "GET UNDER WAY," and "ACT AT DISCRETION." Then she swung across the river and began to drift down, broadside to the current, a performance attributable to Acting Master Wilcox, who thought the ship was getting too close to the starboard shore and ordered the helm put over, without stopping to think that she did not have enough steam to give her steerage way against the current.

At this moment *Manassas* fired her rocket, the fire rafts began to burn, and the Confederate gunnery ships became dimly visible behind. *Vincennes* and *Preble* had cut their cables and got under way in response to the signal in the only manner they could, which was by drifting downstream, an action confirmed by another signal from the flag: "PROCEED DOWN SOUTHWEST PASS."

Lieutenant Francis Winslow of *Water Witch* steamed his ship around through the murk, firing her popguns at anything that could be seen, closing in on *Richmond* from time to time and hailing Pope to persuade him to get his engines going and return upstream. The drift was rapid and the fire rafts were left behind to go aground, but things were now in such a state aboard the flagship that nobody paid any attention to anything until she struck the bar at the river mouth, broadside on and with a slight list. *Vincennes* followed a few minutes later, striking with her stern upstream. *Preble,* which had set some sails, easily got across in response to still another signal from Pope, and so did *Water Witch,* which had not forgotten to take a captured schooner in tow.

*Manassas* had now gone limping back upstream; there was some light from a newly risen moon; and the Confederate gunboats, which had not yet fired a shot, came down to a distance within range of the 9-inch on *McRae* and the small Whitworth rifles of *Ivy* and *Tuscarora*. Captain Robert Handy of *Vincennes* had holes chopped in his ship's stern and two big guns roused round by tackles to fire through them, then thought better of it and sent a boat to Pope with a message:

"Sir: We are aground. We have only two guns that will bear on the enemy.

"Shall I remain on board after the moon goes down with my crippled ship and nearly worn-out crew?

"While we have moonlight would it not be better to leave the ship? Shall I burn her when I leave her?"

Before he could get a reply he had answered his own questions and presently mounted to *Richmond's* deck, incredibly and incongruously draped in an American flag, and announced that he had laid a powder train to *Vincennes'* magazine and set a slow match to it. There was a long wait for the big explosion, during which the Confederate gunboats went away; then inquiry disclosed that although Handy's quarter-gunner had fired the slow match as ordered, he had followed this up by cutting the burning end off and throwing it overboard.

Not a man was hurt in this "battle," and not a shot or shell hit anything except for one of the small Whitworths, which was found next morning in Captain Pope's bureau drawer. He himself described his "retreat" as necessary "to save the ships and prevent them from being sunk and falling into the hands of the enemy." He added that Handy was not fit to command a ship, and remarked that his health was bad, he begged to be allowed to retire, a favor which was accorded him. Next morning most of *Vincennes'* guns and ammunition had to be thrown overboard to get her off the bar, and the Union navy had been effectively driven from the Head of Passes. "I truly feel ashamed for our side," wrote E. F. Devens, exec of *Vincennes,* confi-

dentially to Fox; "the idea of such ships as ours being
driven down the river by nine guns."

Handy was sent north at the time, but later given command of a depot ship at Key West, a singularly light punishment which perhaps reflects influence. Winslow, the
only one who came off with credit, was appointed to the
command of one of the fastest of the new blockading ships,
but died of yellow fever within less than a year.

## VI

At the end of 1861 Mr. Mallory could look at the river
war with reasonable satisfaction. The destructive *Sumter*
had been launched on the seas, and he had four ironclad
rams building, more powerful and less vulnerable than
anything in the Federal service. The emergency ram fleet
was making satisfactory progress and would receive the
cooperation of the Lovell-Montgomery River Defense
Fleet and of the state ships. He had a distinct Confederate
naval triumph at the Head of Passes to report, as against
Belmont, which was regarded as a Union land defeat
instead of a naval victory. It was, in fact, a very creditable
record, except in comparison with the speed of Eads'
building and the power of his ships.

The only thing that really worried Mr. Davis' Secretary
of the Navy was those ships; he believed they could steam
down to New Orleans as soon as complete, and that they
would do so unless prevented by violence.

# 3

# The Day of the Turtle

Two DAYS after Grant's raid on Belmont, Major General Henry Wager Halleck, called "Old Brains," and very fond of scratching his elbows, relieved Frémont in charge of Union armies in the West. He was a most orderly soldier, who did everything by the rules, which meant that he did things slowly. In a military sense he did nothing at all until January of '62, when orders from Washington impelled him to send Grant on reconnaissance in force against Columbus and the twin forts of Henry-Donelson. The object was to keep the Confederates in eastern Kentucky from being reinforced, as there was a prospect of action in that quarter.

One of Grant's division commanders was C. F. Smith, an old warhorse from the fighting in Mexico. As a result of his part of the reconnaissance, he reported it practical to take Fort Heiman with gunboat support. Heiman from its bluffs would command low-lying Henry; with these two in Union hands it would be possible to shoot gunboats up the Tennessee all the way to Mussel Shoals in Alabama, maybe severing the Memphis & Charleston Railroad, that important lateral line of communication. Grant carried the idea to Halleck, who received both him and the proposition frigidly; but Smith's reputation and the backing of Foote won a reluctant permission. Foote and Grant had early established cordial relations; neither one of them liked talking very much.

The release came through on February 1; on February 2 Grant started, using all the laid-up river steamers at Cairo as transports, and even then having only half enough to carry his army. Foote marched on ahead with *Essex, Cincinnati, Carondelet, St. Louis,* and the wooden gunboats, the others being unready for want of men or mechanical adjustments. *There are several ships awaiting crews,* Fox telegraphed from Washington. *You cannot expect men from the navy.*

Grant came upstream with the second echelon; on arrival he found that his divisional commander McClernand had disembarked his men nine miles below Henry, with a wide creek in spate in between and the country around all drowned forest. The general boarded *Essex* to run up and try whether the guns of the fort would permit him to re-embark and land above the creek, and sure enough the shot fired at the gunboat fell short. But just as they were about to turn back for the re-embarkation, a powerful rifled piece opened up, sending a shot right through *Essex* and out the other side, taking the head off a man standing beside Foote.

Grant gazed calmly at the mess and remarked that he guessed McClernand's men had better advance overland.

Meanwhile some of C. F. Smith's division landed on the west bank for the attack on Heiman, but when they closed in found it deserted. It would take so long to get guns in there to shell out Henry that the enemy would have a chance to reinforce; Grant arranged with Foote that Mc-Clernand should close in on the rear of the fort on February 6, while the gunboats attacked it in front. There were some torpedoes in the river; *Tyler* and *Lexington* went on ahead and pulled them up without difficulty during the night.

The 6th was a warm day for February in central Tennessee. The seven ships moved in at the appointed hour, with the ironclads abreast ahead, steaming up a four-mile straight stretch, while the wooden craft came along behind to fire over an island at high angle. Foote came aboard each ship to tell the men not to waste ammunition. "Every charge you fire from those guns costs the government about eight dollars. If your shots fall short you encourage the enemy. If they reach home you demoralize him and get the worth of your money." He shifted his flag to *Cincinnati* that day, which was just as well, as things turned out.

The flagship opened the ball at about a mile distant, and spent $24 worth of shot before *Essex,* elevating more highly, began to hit the parapets. The range was still too long for good practice; with shots from the fort dropping around them, the gunboats moved in to 500 yards, steadied at that point on their wheels, and, both sides being in good range, the firing was general. It kept up for over an hour, a persistent cannonade by dead green but determined men on both sides. At the half-hour a shell smashed *Essex'* pilothouse; at the three-quarter mark another pierced the port casemate and detonated in the boiler, with three men killed and 29 scalded so badly that almost all died, Bill

Porter of the foxy face and long beard being one of the survivors. Nine of the dead were borrowed army artillerists.

By this time the fort was a good deal worn. General Lloyd Tilghman in command had sent most of his men overland to Donelson in view of the coming land encirclement, which he lacked the troops to resist. The wind whipped across the stream, blowing smoke away from the ships and making their gunnery excellent. The barracks were burning and piles of timber in the fort area; the big Parrott rifle, his best gun, was hit near the muzzle just as its lanyard was pulled, and blew up, killing most of the crew; the large Columbiad was filled with earth by a shell that burst just short of it. Now the gunboats closed in still more, giving two of the 32-pounders direct hits at the same moment, and disabling every man at both. There were now only four guns able to fire, each cut down to about one shot in ten minutes by damage to internal communications. General Tilghman thought he had better surrender and was only delayed by halyards fouled around the flagstaff. When Grant's men arrived Tilghman was already aboard *Cincinnati,* being treated to a drink as a "gentlemanly person." The flag had been hit 31 times, *Essex* 15, *St. Louis* seven, and *Carondelet* six, but *Essex* was the only one that really suffered, and the capacity of Eads' gunboats to deal with forts was well and truly demonstrated.

Grant's reaction was to telegraph Halleck that he intended to "take and destroy Fort Donelson," then cut the wires lest "Old Brains" order him back and start marching. Foote's was to borrow some soldiers to fill out the crews of two more of Eads' gunboats for the assault, and meanwhile (at Grant's request) to order Phelps with the three wooden ships to go as far as he could up the Tennessee and to damage anything he could find. There was never any trouble between Grant and Foote, although the naval officer did send a *sotto-voce* grumble to Washington about being so thoroughly under Army that "every brigadier can interfere with me."

Phelps and his ships made a long, surprisingly fast cruise up the Tennessee. Somewhere near the mouth of the Duck River they came on three transports, loaded with military stores and ammunition and, after a chase, found them burning. They blew up with such violence that skylights were broken, doors slammed open, and aboard *Conestoga* the upper deck lifted from its supports. At Cerro Gordo, reached on February 7, was the river steamer *Eastport,* which the rebels had begun to convert into an ironclad but had carried only to the point of cutting down her upper decks and building a slanting casemate, like that on the Pook ships, to receive plating. She had been scuttled and her suction pipes broken, but she was a bigger ship than *Benton,* and the sabotage was so recent that the water had no time to damage her seriously. Phelps' experienced rivermen patched the leaks, and *Lexington* towed her downstream to Cairo to be completed for service under the old flag. Two more steamers were destroyed at Chickasaw, and another three just at Mussel Shoals, where Phelps added to the enemy's logistic problem by burning all the lumber piles and sawmills in the neighborhood; a terrifying, if temporary breakage was made in the big lateral railroad running east from Memphis.

On February 7 in the morning Grant sent Walke, with *Carondelet* and a company of infantry some dozen miles up the Tennessee to make sure of knocking out the drawbridge on the Memphis and Bowling Green line; it had already received a certain amount of battering from the wooden ships, but might conceivably be repaired in time to let the rebels reinforce Donelson from Memphis. When the ship returned to communication, Grant desired Walke to feel out Donelson from the river, Foote being back at Cairo to get more gunboats ready. The current in the Cumberland was swift; the transport *Alps* had to lend a hand in towing *Carondelet* to position, half-hidden by a wooded point, about a mile from the fort, on the morning of February 13.

The gunboat steadied herself and opened a deliberate fire, which was kept up until evening with an interval for lunch and clearing wounded to *Alps,* or until most of the ammunition had been spent. The range was beyond that of the 32's in the fort and only the two big guns fired. The damage to the ship was one shot from a 48-pound rifle, which came through the armor forward and flew around inside, distributing small splinters that wounded 11 men, most of them very lightly. The damage to Donelson was one of the 9-pounders out of action and the Columbiad hit so that it would not traverse well. None of this was visible.

At eleven-thirty that night Foote arrived, in a rather bad temper and inclined to be short. The parson had been late at church the previous Sunday morning and he had to take the pulpit and deliver the exhortation himself—to the text, *"Ye believe in God, also believe in me,"* and in such a manner that the congregation interpreted it as: *"Ye believe in God, believe also in the gunboats."* He had been forced to cannibalize damaged *Cincinnati* for men in addition to drawing on the army to fill out the crews of *Pittsburg* and *Louisville,* which he had brought upstream with *St. Louis* (the flag), *Tyler,* and *Conestoga.*

Grant wanted Foote to attack the fort the following afternoon in conjunction with a bombardment by land artillery, and although Foote considered his squadron disjointed and far from ready, he made his plan at once and on the basis of previous experience. Henry had been smothered by the ships' fire from short range, and Walke reported *Carondelet* had not done too well from afar; let us close in then, and beat the batteries down. The ironclads would take the lead, in line abreast; the two wooden ships follow at a thousand yards, firing shells at high angle. All the "hard materials," bags of coal, lumber, chains, were piled on the unprotected upper decks as protection against the plunging fire of high-mounted guns.

The ships went up the river with *Louisville, St. Louis, Pittsburg, Carondelet,* from left to right, spacing the experienced hands with the new. Sure enough, the new hands fell behind and Foote had to order them by megaphone to: "Steam up." At 3:00 P.M. and a mile and a half from the fort, two shots were fired from it, both short. Foote kept calmly pushing in and at 2000 yards opened fire from all ships. He kept on driving and did not steady until he was 400 yards from the fort, at which point not only the 32s but the carronades and even the remaining 9-pounder would bear.

Now the ships had to take a heavy plunging fire. One of *Carondelet's* big forward guns blew up because the men loaded it too rapidly; several of the crew were killed; and another found himself "stepping in blood and brains on the deck." At 200 yards from the fort, the question of who was smothering whom remained undecided and the ships were having trouble reaching the heights. Mr. Joseph Mc-

Cullagh, reporter for the Cincinnati *Gazette,* in the pilothouse of *St. Louis,* heard a terrible crash as a shell broke
through and exploded. He looked around; the wheel had
disappeared and the pilot, "with what seemed a wonder-
ing, questioning expression," slowly melted to the deck,
a huge splinter through his chest, and was dead before
help could be summoned. One of Foote's legs was smashed
at the ankle and the flagship was drifting downstream, hit
65 times and with the damage in the pilothouse by no
means the only casualties.

At almost the same time both *Pittsburg* and *Louisville*
had their wheel ropes shot away, and were prevented from
using their tillers by shells from the wooden ships with
fuses cut too short, which were bursting over them instead
of in the fort. The pair joined *St. Louis* in drifting downstream and away; *Carondelet* maintained the contest singlehanded for an hour more, with the men shouting
"Down!" and ducking behind the guns as the big pieces
in Donelson flashed. Then she pulled out, with 54 hits,
several of them on the waterline, which made her leak
so badly she had to go back to Mound City for a long
period of repairs.

That is, the attack was definitely, decidedly, a failure.
Everything in this river war was to learn, and on this
occasion Foote learned that the water-level guns of Henry
were something quite different from the high-mounted
guns at Donelson, and that you did not bring a few heavy
pieces into range of more numerous light ones. Also he
made no attempt (being perhaps excusable because of his
early and painful wound) to run even one of the ships
past the fort and blockade it from upstream. For this lack
about 5000 of the garrison got away in boats across the

river before the place surrendered to Grant's land attack, two days later.

But above the tactical failure at Donelson soared the tremendous strategic success of the combined operation. Not only was the whole Confederate system of river defense with fortifications vitiated by demonstration; but also the center of the strategic line west of the mountains was broken, all Kenucky and middle Tennessee recovered to the Union, Polk's fortress at Columbus outflanked, and an entire army dispersed or taken, the loss of whose manpower was to be bitterly felt. Grant deserves all the credit, yes; but the river navy put him where he could gain it. It is only necessary to ask what would have happened to the campaign had the Pook turtles been on the other side.

The fall of the double fortresses brought about a revision of Confederate strategic planning. The Memphis & Charleston Railroad was felt to be a strategic necessity and a new line of defense was organized to cover it, with the right at Chattanooga, the center at Corinth, and the left resting on Fort Pillow and Memphis. Island No. 10 was to be held as a projection of the left wing; it should keep the abolitionists from coming down the Mississippi and throwing the campaign inland. Polk was ordered to move 140 of his heavy guns to that point and Pillow, but to keep his men in hand for mobile operations. Not all the artillery had time to make the trip.

## II

Halleck, who did not realize that he was dealing with a war beyond the European chessboard pattern, condemned Grant for not making proper ration returns and forbade the remaining gunboats to go beyond Clarksville; but by time they got the orders they had already taken Nashville and were poking still farther up the Cumberland.

Meanwhile, on an earlier suggestion from Fox, Frémont had laid down at the Carondelet 14 "mortar rafts," long hexagons in trace, 60 by 25 feet, with sloping seven-foot timber bulwarks 17 inches thick and iron-plated, each carrying a 13-inch mortar, to be towed into position for long-range bombardment missions. When the mortar was loaded, the crew slipped through a door at one end and stood outside on the deck till it was fired. There were many doubts whether the vessels would stand the recoil, but three of the gunboat captains fired the first one and she took no damage, so Foote assembled ten of these vessels and went downstream with four ironclads and transports carrying 1000 troops for a look at Columbus.

He was met by a flag of truce and a message from General Polk, hoping "that the courtesies he had extended to captured Union officers would be reciprocated." Foote's bad leg, the curious position in which the white flag placed him, and Grant's idea that Columbus would have to be given up without fighting because it was outflanked, deterred the Flag Officer from attack. He was back at Cairo on February 23, completing and finding crews for the remaining gunboats, since there were tales of a powerful Confederate river flotilla farther down.

The wooden gunboats stayed in the lesser streams. Nelson's division of Buell's Army of the Cumberland went up to Nashville under convoy of *Conestoga* late in February. Buell himself arrived, feeling so nervous about the position that he called on C. F. Smith's division of Grant for help against attack, but the rebels liked the heavy guns of Foote's ships so little that they pulled out and there was really nothing for the troops to do.

Tennessee was so thoroughly divided in loyalties that neither side had much trouble getting quick intelligence. It was brought to the attention of Bill Gwin, commanding *Tyler,* that the Confederates were fortifying Pittsburg Landing, the point on the Tennessee where debarkation was usually made to transship from river traffic to Corinth on the Memphis & Charleston Railroad. On March 1 Gwin, without any orders except his own inspiration, ran up the Tennessee with his own ship and Shirk's *Lexington,* arriving the next day.

The rebels had some eight guns in position, none of which could have been over 9-pounders, since they were field pieces, although a few of them were rifles. These were clearly no match for the 8-inch and 32-pounders of the gunboats; within a few minutes the batteries had been shelled out and their men were flying, while troops landed from the gunboats scouted around to find out everything they could about the area.

As a military affair this was very small potatoes indeed, but it was one of the cases where great strategic effects grew from a potato's eye. Gwin's report, enthusiastically endorsed by Foote, told Mr. Welles that the crews of the gunboats would be protected against musketry from the shore, while their own ordnance would be heavy enough to cover them against any guns the Confederates could move around. Someone, most probably Pook,[1] suggested that river steamers could do the job if merely cut down and sheathed with boiler-iron instead of receiving the elaborate reconstruction Rodgers had given his timberclads.

[1] It is not certain, because the matter was settled verbally without a recorder and Welles had not begun to write his famous diary at the time. But it was not Chief Constructor Lenthall; he was uninterested in anything that had iron on it.

For the moment this was of none effect, but events presently called for the decision to be reviewed, and out of it grew the most numerous class of ships the U. S. Navy possessed down to the days of the World Wars—the "tin-clads," built to "run on a heavy dew" and penetrate far up the inland rivers. They were altered river ships all, and admirable vessels on which virile young lieutenants could gain experience and get into trouble. The conversions were made in all the river ports, principally Pittsburgh, Mound City, Cincinnati, and St. Louis; they were as various and peculiar as their names and armaments. Only *Black Hawk,* 902 tons, was of any size, and she was rather specially fitted out as flagship and floating office.

On March 4 Foote was ready for another go at Columbus and steamed down with *Benton, Mound City, Louisville, Carondelet, Cincinnati, St. Louis, Pittsburg,* and *Lexington,* taking five of the mortar rafts and a contingent of troops on four transports with a number of tugs and lighters. The expedition was set for a fight, but it proved unnecessary; the place had been taken the day before by a company of cavalry from Paducah and the Union flag was floating on the ramparts.

With Grant and Buell both concentrating toward the Tennessee for a blow at Corinth, the abandonment of Columbus had the command effect of transferring control of Foote's squadron to General John Pope, no relation of the "Honest John" who got himself in trouble at the Head of Passes. Pope had organized the forces in Missouri to the extent of 17,000 men and was working slowly down the right bank of the stream. Some eight miles above Island No. 10 there was a check; the hard ground gave way to a complete squash of tree-grown swamp, several feet deep in water. The Kentucky-Tennessee side was just as bad down to the point where there began the riverside strip of hard ground which held the batteries facing Island No. 10. There was no approach except by the river.

Below the island the Missouri side also has a ribbon of high ground. General Pope perceived that if the swamps behind the high banks prevented access to the fort by land, they would also inhibit supply and escape if the banks below the fort were taken. He directed his engineers to build a road across the neck above Island No. 10 to New Madrid. They pointed out that the river was in freshet and so were all the tributaries called bayous that run through the swamps behind the banks; any road they built would be suitable only for men on ten-foot stilts, but they could give him a dandy canal. Build the canal, then, said Pope; they did so by means of an ingenious sawing machine that cut off trunks under water, and by March 19 enough men and artillery were floated through on barges to place the Union in possession of New Madrid.

Meanwhile Foote brought his fleet and mortar boats down on March 17 for a try at bombardment. The gunboats had to shoot from at anchor and from a range long enough to make their armor proof, since any damage to their engines would have brought them drifting helpless down under the guns, and an experiment with *Carondelet* had demonstrated that she could not be steadied sufficiently to fire well while backing against the current. During the shoot *Benton* was hit four times without penetration, but the fire of the ships was clearly ineffective and there was nothing to indicate what results the mortars were getting.

The next day and the next and the one after that the mortars pounded away monotonously. Then came a request from General Pope. He needed an armored gunboat below the forts; the light field pieces he had been able to

float through the canal would not reach the similar batteries the Confederates had on the Tennessee side below
the forts and he could not cross until the latter were elim-
inated. Foote said it would be destruction for one of his
lightly armored ships to try running down, and the long-
range firing of ships and mortars went on.

On the 28th Pope was back at Foote, more insistent
than ever, reminding the naval officer that the rebels had
a pair of powerful ironclads building at Memphis, which
might at any time lead the enemy river fleet upstream
to drive Union men and guns from their positions along
the Missouri shore. Their lighter vessels were already
shelling his downriver flank from a distance where they
could not be reached. Foote called a formal council of
war, with every captain present; all but the impatient and
thorny Walke said no gunboat could run the batteries,
whereupon Foote asked Walke if he would care to do it,
and, getting an affirmative, told him to prepare.

The first danger point was Battery No. 1, an 11-gun
installation two miles above the main forts. Against this,
Foote dispatched by night the boats of the fleet with 50
volunteers from the 42nd Illinois. On the night of April 1
they slid in close, boarded over slippery mud ramparts
with a shout, and found that luck was with them. The
place had become so uncomfortable from high water that
the rebels were manning it only when firing and there
were few aboard. The guns were spiked or tumbled from
their mounts, and there was little chance that the battery
could be brought back to function under mortar fire.

Now came the floating battery, or fighting dry dock,
moored in the stream at the head of the Island. Next
morning all the gunboats and mortars concentrated on it,
and it was soon evident that however well ordered it was

to hold off level fire, the plunging bombs of the mortars were a different matter. The rebels had to cut their lashings and let the monster drift downstream to a position and in a condition that made it innocuous.

Walke piled everything he could find on his upper deck as a defense against plunging shot, wound hawsers and chain cable around the inadequately armored pilothouse, and lashed a coal barge filled with hay to *Carondelet's* port side. Cordwood was piled around the boilers inboard; the escape steam was piped through the wheelhouse to avoid the normal puffing noise. "She looks like a farmer's wagon," commented the skipper ruefully; but at ten o'clock on the night of April 4 the moon had set and a thunderstorm shot with lightning was blowing in. The little ironclad cast off and began to move downstream with First Master William B. Hoel on the foredeck to con her and Seaman Charles Wilson, knee-deep in foaming water and with the storm beating round his head, to heave the lead.

She steamed like a shade through thunder and blazing lightning till just past the first batteries, when the soot in her smokestacks, deprived of its usual wetting by the escape steam, caught fire and picked her out with two long pennons of illumination. There were shouts and bugles from the forts; before the fire was out the guns began to crash, and aboard they could hear officers shouting: "Elevate! Elevate!" But in the dark and among the flashes *Carondelet* was an elusive target; it is likely that no gun had more than two cracks at her and the projectiles only streamed past without touching. Hoel saved her with his conning, or she would have gone aground; she reached New Madrid at midnight and began firing minute-guns to announce success, while Pope's staff rolled out a barrel of red-eye to celebrate. There was one cannonball in the coal barge and one in a bale of hay.

That was the story. On the 6th, after a day of rest, *Carondelet* began shelling out Confederate batteries, and since there was another thunderstorm that night, Foote sent *Pittsburg* through to join her. Next afternoon the two gunboats killed off more batteries and began carrying Pope's men to the Tennessee side; before sunset Island No. 10 and 7000 soldiers surrendered to the navy. The general got all the credit at the time, but it was really *Carondelet's* victory and Walke's. More important, another defect had been introduced into the syllogism of Confederate strategy; forts could not stop ironclads if the latter merely wished to shoulder past.

## III

On March 1 Halleck sent Grant orders to strike at Corinth and directed Buell's Army of the Cumberland to come help. There was some cross-purpose of orders, reports, and complaints that has no part in this story, but the total effect was that in the latter days of March, Grant began to concentrate around Pittsburg Landing, the point from which the Confederates had been driven by *Tyler* and *Lexington*. The same two gunboats covered his transports.

Albert Sidney Johnston, Confederate commander in the West, was perfectly conscious of this movement and thoroughly determined to strike a blow that would break the Union forces opposing his center before they could reach the Memphis & Charleston Railroad. He formed a concentration of everything west of the mountains and east of the Mississippi, and his scouting being much better than that of the Union commander, was able to attack at six o'clock in the morning of Sunday, April 6, and to obtain surprise. The tale of the confused and rowdy Battle of Shiloh, the most desperate fighting America had yet seen, through intricate woods by green troops, belongs to another kind of history. What matters here is that the Confederates began to drive the Union left wing, and if they could drive it far enough to take the landing, Grant's army would be spun off into the woods and utterly lost.

General Johnston was killed in the drive, but General Bragg took over, reorganized, and got the Confederate lines moving forward on the vital wing. At about three in the afternoon Bill Gwin steamed up with *Tyler,* opened an enfilading fire, and in about 35 minutes had disorganized two Confederate brigades and put their artillery out of business. At this point it occurred to him that he was entering action without authorization; he stopped and sent his gunner to Grant to ask instructions. The general, who already had three bullet holes through his clothes and a horse shot under him, told Gwin to use his judgment.

Gwin's judgment was that every time a gun fired from the thickets it should get a few from the 32's. The heavy guns, using grape and canister, had entirely too much spread, and before five o'clock the Confederate assaults on the Union left had ceased and their General Beauregard (who had now taken over from Bragg) was sending his men into bivouac. At six *Tyler* began firing 5- and 10-second fused shell over the banks to the limit of range, which proved very discouraging to the rebels, who could make no reply. By six-twenty-five the Confederate attacks had ceased, but at 9:00 P.M. Nelson came in with his division of Buell and told Gwin to shoot away. All night the two gunboats drenched the enemy lines with 5-, 10-, and 15-second shell, one relieving the other. Few in the Confederate lines could sleep under that iron hail and they had been fighting since dawn; when Grant and Buell violently counterattacked on the Monday morning, the enemy broke, the battle was won, and the fate of the Memphis and Charleston sealed.

No one would claim that the gunboats won the battle. That was Grant and Sherman, the timely arrival of Buell's steady battalions, and the resolution of the soldiers of the Army of the Tennessee. But *Tyler* and *Lexington* provided heavy artillery support (which always ruins field artillery in counterbattery) at a crucial moment in a crucial place, and demonstrated that no Union army which rested its flank on a river where there were gunboats need worry about the safety of that flank.

# 4

## *Unexpected*

O N NOVEMBER 12, 1861, Commander David Dixon Porter
arrived in Washington from the Gulf, feeling "like a cat
in a strange garret." A little over seven months before,
on the authority of Secretary Seward, he had run off to
Pensacola with the powerful side-wheel frigate *Powhatan,*
instead of using her for the relief of Fort Sumter, as
ordered by Navy, and now he was not at all sure of his
reception. But he had an idea, Assistant Navy Secretary
Fox was a close personal friend, and the moment was
rendered specially propitious by the headlines in the
morning papers, which told of the capture of Port Royal
and its forts by a Union naval squadron.

In Mr. Welles' anteroom Senators Grimes and Hale of
the naval committee were waiting to offer their congratu-
lations on the victory. Porter explained his plan to them—
nothing less than to send a seaborne expedition against

71

New Orleans, largest city and chief port of the Confederacy. The variety of exits and the close approach of
sounds and lakes above the delta made it impossible to
keep the place under proper blockade. What about the
great river forts, Jackson and St. Philip? They could be
battered into insensibility, said Porter, by 48 hours' fire
from heavy mortars at a distance, and under that cover a
fleet mounting 200 guns could easily run past to take the
city; the forts, cut off, would have to surrender.

At this point they were admitted to the Secretary, all
going in together. Welles received Porter with a cordiality
which surprised the naval officer, who did not know that
the Secretary's special vanity was not letting his estimate
of anyone as a person interfere with his judgment on
capacities. Porter made his explanation over again and
Welles remarked that such a project had been considered
since September, without anyone suggesting a valid *modus
operandi*. After the senators left, Assistant Secretary Fox
was called in and the whole caravan went to see Lincoln.
The President, as a man who knew his river, was equally
easy to impress and arranged for a conference that evening
with General McClellan, lately appointed Commander-
in-Chief of the army, since this was a deal that would
involve troops.

At the evening meeting McClellan greeted Porter as an
old friend, but expressed doubts about the plan. Wooden
ships would be crushed like eggshells trying to get past
heavily casemated Fort Jackson; the operation would re-
quire a siege by at least 50,000 troops, which could not be
spared from the Army of the Potomac. Welles rode down
the last objection by remarking that 10,000 would be
plenty in addition to the 2500 General Ben Butler was
raising in Massachusetts, already specifically earmarked

for Gulf service. The conference became one on planning
how to keep the operation a secret, since surprise would
be two thirds of the game. It would be impossible to hide
the preparations for so large an expedition; all agreed that
the true destination would be covered by setting up a new
blockading squadron in the West Gulf and talking earnestly about Pensacola, Mobile, Savannah, Charleston, or
even Galveston—anything but New Orleans.

Welles and Porter collaborated in drawing a list of ships
for the expedition. The next question was selecting a
commander. It seems to have been Fox who suggested
David Glasgow Farragut, Porter's adoptive brother, 60
years old and 37th on the list of captains, now on a retire-
ment board, but a man who had demonstrated that, unlike
such senior officers as Honest John Pope, he had not forgotten that the first duty of a naval captain is to fight.
The only trouble was that he came from Tennessee and
had lived many years in Norfolk. How did he feel? Porter
was dispatched to see Farragut in Brooklyn and find out.

The conversation began with Porter asking what the
older man thought of the officers who had resigned to join
the Confederacy.

"Those damned fellows will catch it yet!" said Farragut.

"I am glad to hear you say that. Will you accept a command, such as no officer in the navy ever held, to go and
fight those fellows whose conduct you so reprobate?"

"What do you mean?" asked the old man.

"I will tell you nothing until you have answered my
questions," said Porter, and led the conversation in a way
to suggest that Norfolk, Farragut's wife's home and that
of many of his friends, would be the object of attack. The
badgered captain finally said he would serve "honestly and
faithfully without any mental reservations," then jumped

from his seat, crying: "I will take the command, only don't you trifle with me!"

Porter was the kind of man who could later set the incident down as exquisitely humorous, but he knew he had his commander, and Farragut was invited to Washington for a breakfast with Fox at the home of Postmaster General Montgomery Blair. After the preliminaries were over Farragut was asked for a purely advisory opinion on whether New Orleans could be taken from the sea.

"Yes, emphatically," said the old man. "The forts are well down the river; ships could easily run them and New Orleans itself is undefended. It would depend somewhat on the fleet, however."

Fox: "Well, with such a fleet as, say, two steam frigates, five screw sloops of the cities class, a dozen 90-day gunboats and some mortar vessels to shell the forts from high angle?"

Farragut: "Why, I would engage to run those batteries with two thirds of such a force. Leave out the mortars, though; they only delay things."

Fox: "What would you say if appointed to head such an expedition?"

"What would I say?" cried Farragut, leaping to his feet and prowling the room like a cat, the whole scheme now becoming clear. "What would I say?" and burst into expressions of delight.

After he had left, Blair gently stroked his sideburns and wondered if the commodore were not too enthusiastic. Fox thought not; the gasconade was all on the surface; the man was determined, energetic, and discreet.

Of course, part of this advocacy was due to the eupeptic, black-bearded Porter, who had already been appointed to head the mortar flotilla and who, in his own mind, would be the real chief of the expedition, with his aging foster-brother under his dominance. This was the basic reason why Farragut's suggestion about leaving out the mortars, reinforced next day by letter, never got anywhere, although the official version was that Porter had already purchased some of the 20 schooners to be converted to mortar vessels and ordered the guns to be cast in Pittsburgh. The beds for them were to be made there too, but the constructors were too busy with work for the river fleet. Farragut himself finally placed the order with Cooper & Hewitt of New York on January 23 and got his beds on February 8, which is something remarkable in speed of construction.

Farragut received his official orders on December 23 and began fitting out at once. The fleet finally shaped up as consisting of a big steam frigate of 50 guns, one of the most powerful warships in the world, in modern terms a battle-cruiser; four heavy screw sloops with 24 9-inch Dahlgrens[1] each, a pair of 6-inch rifles and 2 howitzers; a side-wheel frigate with a 10-inch and 15 8-inch; three large screw gunboats with varying armaments of 6 to 10 guns, 11-inch to 30-pounder rifles; and nine of those remarkable 90-day gunboats with an 11-inch, a light rifle and 2 howitzers apiece—total, 243 guns as against the 200 originally proposed by Porter. In addition the sailing sloop *Portsmouth,* with 16 8-inch was taken along to provide gunnery cover for the mortar schooners in case they met a raider on the sea, and the revenue cutter *Harriet Lane,* with five ferryboats as tows for the schooners.[2]

[1] Named for their inventor, Captain John A. Dahlgren, the ordnance expert; they were thickest in the area of greatest pressure and therefore somewhat bottle-shaped.

[2] The full roster was: frigate *Colorado* (Captain Theodorus Bailey); first-class screw sloops *Hartford* (Commander Richard Wainwright, with Captain H. H. Bell aboard as "flag captain," which was substantially

Farragut hoisted his flag in *Hartford* at Philadelphia on
January 19, 1862, and dropped down to Hampton Roads,
where he found final letters of instruction, telling him to
"take advantage of the panic" the capture of New Orleans
would cause and "push a strong force up the river to take
all their defenses in the rear," after which he was to go to
Mobile, reduce its forts, and turn them over to the army,
as though the whole program were a matter of weeks. At
Key West on February 11, he found *Pensacola,* with her
engines in poor shape, and six of Porter's bombs. Talks
and an examination of charts convinced him that there
was a constant trickle of small blockade-runners out of
the lakes and bayous of the whole West Gulf coast, now
under his charge, and that oceangoing navy ships could
not deal with them. He wrote Welles urgently, asking for
vessels of not more than five-foot draft, which could carry
2 or 3 20-pounder rifles, as well as for more medical men
and mechanics.

Farragut forgot to specify that the light-draft ships were
wanted for blockade rather than the river attack, and Fox
failed to understand, which produced a highly revelatory
dividend of correspondence. Fox to Porter:

We have dispatches from your Flag, a cold shudder ran
through me at the time. He wants a lot of 4-foot draft boats.
This is not the time for such requests— There are no boats

---

chief of staff), *Brooklyn* (Captain T. T. Craven), *Richmond* (Captain James
Alden), *Pensacola* (Captain Henry W. Morris); side-wheel frigate *Missis-
sippi* (Commander T. O. Selfridge); lighter screw sloops *Oneida* (Com-
mander S. P. Lee), *Varuna* (Commander Charles S. Boggs), *Iroquois*
(Commander John De Camp); with the 90-day gunboats *Cayuga* (Lieuten-
ant N. B. Harrison), *Katahdin* (Lieutenant George H. Preble) , *Kennebec*
(Lieutenant John B. Russell), *Kineo* (Lieutenant George M. Ransom),
*Pinola* (Lieutenant Pierce Crosby), *Sciota* (Lieutenant Edward Donaldson),
*Winona* (Lieutenant Edward T. Nichols), *Wissahickon* (Lieutenant A. M.
Smith).

under 7-foot draft and they are good for nothing, and if he does the work laid out for him there will be no use for these frail boats, not one of which would get to the Gulf at this season of the year. I trust we have made no mistake in our man but his dispatches are very discouraging. It is not too late to rectify our mistake. You must frankly give me your views from Ship Island. I shall have no peace until I hear from you.

When Porter got the letter, he had already passed the rendezvous at Ship Island, some 30 miles south of Biloxi in Mississippi Sound, had had several contacts with the old senior captains who commanded the big sloops, and had achieved a state of incandescence. He answered:

If you suppose there is any want of the proper abilities in the Flag Officer it is now too late to rectify the mistake. I never thought Farragut a Nelson or a Collingwood; I only considered him the best of his rank and so consider him still; but men of his age in a seafaring life are not fit for important enterprises, they lack the vigor of youth. He talks very much at random at times and rather underrates the difficulties before him without fairly comprehending them. I know what they are, and as he is impressible hope to make him appreciate them also. I have great hopes of the mortars if all else fails.

That is, there were undercurrents. Porter made his separate supply arrangements for his mortars, failed to give a roster of their officers to Farragut, in all respects treating his own as a separate force and corresponding directly with his gossip Fox as though he were some kind of seeing-eye dog for the infirm old flag officer and the aging captains. In addition Farragut found only 400 tons of coal at Ship Island, not nearly enough, and discovered that no medical supplies or bandages at all had been furnished him. Around his head blew a snowstorm of paperwork, most of it trivial, and he had trouble with his eyes. He had to arrange for and supervise repairs to *Pensacola's* engines and take up the unhappy fact that when the rebel ram *Manassas* came down Pas à l'Outre and grounded just inside, in plain sight of *Mississippi,* Captain Selfridge[3] did not fire a gun. Selfridge was sent home and the ship given to Commander Melancton Smith.

Yet the work went forward. On March 7 Farragut arrived at Pas à l'Outre with *Brooklyn* and *Hartford,* failed to get through the silt, and went round to Southwest Pass, where, on the 16th, both ships got into the river by careening. Some of the gunboats had already preceded him and taken possession of the Head of Passes, with its shanty village of Pilot Town, which was inhabited chiefly by an Italian oyster-pickler, making it into a temporary base. On the 18th Porter, his ferryboats having arrived after a tempestuous trip, towed all the schooners across the bar at Pas à l'Outre, took them up to the Head of Passes, where they discharged their seagoing spars and made ready.

It was clear that the huge frigate *Colorado,* with her 23-foot draft, could never get across the bar, and *Mississippi* and *Pensacola,* the deepest of the others, only with difficulty. All three were sent back to Ship Island, *Colorado* to have some of her guns taken out for distribution among other ships, *Mississippi* and *Pensacola* to be relieved of some of their heavier weights for the passage.

When they came back to Southwest Pass, Porter brought his towboats down and began to haul *Mississippi* through; she made it on April 4, an inch at a time and after four days of labor. But Captain Morris of *Pensacola* waved the

[3] This was not the Selfridge who did so well with the Mississippi gunboats, but his father, one of the old senior captains.

tows aside and steamed his ship at the bar full speed and vomiting smoke. She ran hard on the mud and a sunken wreck, and it took days to get her out again into deep water. Porter vowed he would have nothing more to do with her and got off an exasperated letter to Fox, saying that the big sloops should be commanded by young lieutenants instead of old and talkative captains; Farragut (he said) lacked control. "The rank is now so near alike that a Flag Officer has no force, and every old fogy out here is trying to play commander if left a day to himself."

That was how it looked to Porter. Farragut remained calm; when Morris told him of Porter's refusal to tow his sloop up and asked that an order be issued to the energetic subordinate, the commander-in-chief refused glacially, told Morris he would have to eat humble pie and present his own request, and went out on deck to turn his usual handspring for morning exercise. He was making a first-class impression through the squadron and was conscious of it. Early in the morning he would have himself rowed from ship to ship, conversing with the duty officers, cheerful and self-confident, floating all spirits over a fairly general agreement that they could never pass the forts.

The organization moved smoothly under the hands of tall, straight Captain Bell, though Porter thought the man a booby. Theodorus Bailey of *Colorado* did not wish to be left out of the fighting because his ship was, and was made second in command, with the assignment of leading the line when the fleet moved upstream. B. S. Osbon, correspondent of the New York *Herald,* was not allowed to send dispatches until something decisive had happened, so became a kind of unofficial admiral's clerk. On April 7, with careening and difficulty, *Pensacola* was put through;

on the 14th the oceangoing vessels, rerigged, rearmed, and supplied with bandages borrowed from Butler's army forces (which were 18,000 instead of the promised 12,500) moved up the river.

Farragut had prepared the most detailed orders; all spars down to topmast were to be landed and fore rigging cleared for better end-on fire; howitzers to be mounted in the fore and main tops; grapnels ready for towing off fire-ships. Each vessel was to be trimmed slightly by the head, so that if she went aground she would not swing stern upstream. Methods of stopping shot-holes and serving guns in battle were detailed. By an idea due to Engineer Moore of *Richmond*, an iron rod was fastened to the side of each ship with I-bolts about eight feet above the water and chain cables looped over as a kind of armor. Chain cables were piled around the steam drums and the bows filled up with cables of hemp. A coastal survey vessel ran up to post markers under the fire of snipers in the swamps, and the great adventure was about to begin, even though the supplies of ammunition and especially of coal were far short of what they should have been.

## II

The Confederate intelligence service was both too good and nowhere near as good as it needed to be. It furnished elaborate accurate information about the Eads ironclads building at St. Louis and Mound City, which convinced Mallory that New Orleans was in grave danger from Foote's fleet upstream; it also convinced him (thanks to the Washington precautions about rumor-spreading) that Farragut was going to Mobile or Galveston. This was a defective evaluation; any real naval man could have told

Mallory that the mortars (of whose fitting out he was well aware) would have been useless against either of the coastal cities. But no one did tell him and in the early months of 1862 he ordered everything up to Memphis, the Hollins navy ships, the Montgomery flotilla, and, as soon as she was finished, the ironclad *Louisiana*.

At this time Lovell's own opinion jelled with his. On February 27 the general, with full knowledge of what was going on in the Gulf, was writing: "I regard Butler's Ship Island expedition as a harmless menace so far as New Orleans is concerned." The March flood that took out the first boom dissolved some of this confidence; there began to be conversations among naval and military men in the city as to whether the forts could be passed, with much learned discussion of the effect of heavy shell-firing guns on wooden ships at close range, something as yet not tried in war. A good many took pessimism and agreed with Governor Moore that the forts could hold out only as long as the new boom. J. K. Mitchell and William C. Whittle, whose command relations as head of the New Orleans naval station, and the naval force, have never been satisfactorily deciphered, began sending telegrams of apprehension to Richmond. Their fears presently infected Hollins and Lovell was induced to keep part of the Montgomery fleet downstream.

On April 6, when all Farragut's ships except *Pensacola* were across the bar, Whittle fairly got the wind up and wired Hollins at Memphis, without even consulting the Navy Department; he wanted everything afloat to come down to New Orleans at once. Hollins himself started in *Ivy*, but felt he needed confirmation and wired Mallory— the enemy had passed and taken Island No. 10, he could do nothing to arrest their progress on the upper river, while he might do a great deal to stop the ocean ships coming upstream. The reply was categorical:

Your dispatch received yesterday proposed to abandon opposition to the enemy's descent of the river by your fleet and to carry your fleet to the mouth of the river. This proposition it totally inadmissible; every effort that nautical skill, invention, and courage can be put forth must be made to oppose the enemy's descent of the river, and at every hazard. You inform me that you have gone to New Orleans at the urgent request of Captain Whittle. You will therefore send these orders to the senior in command of your squadron by telegraph. The *Louisiana* must join your squadron at the earliest possible moment.

But *Louisiana* was at that moment in no condition to join anything. She had developed the defects of any great machine designed in haste by men without any experience in this particular business. The portholes were so small that the guns could only be elevated four or five degrees and could hardly be trained at all; the steering propellers were not ready for use and the rudder was helpless to steer her by itself; the anchor purchases were so weak that the hooks could not be lifted once they were down; the crew was a scratch collection of army artillerists; there was no place for the officers to sleep except in tents on top of the casemate—and worst of all, the engines borrowed from *Ingomar* would not work, not at all. As Farragut crossed the bar, *Louisiana's* whole inner economy was filled with mechanics, trying to persuade those engines to go. They never succeeded.

*Mississippi* had been launched and her timberwork was complete, but the vital 50-foot central shaft was still missing and she was only armored below the gundeck. Governor Moore complained later that the Tifts refused offered aid in men and money, but this seems to have been because they had all the men who could be employed working days, and nobody would take a night shift.

As Federal survey boats pushed up the river, tying rags to branches and setting others on poles along the stream, General Johnson K. Duncan, commanding the forts, sent out parties of sharpshooters to snipe at them and tear down the markers. As an operation this was not quite a success; the men had to stand in water to their waists or shoulders and when they fired, a gunboat would deluge the whole area with shrapnel from howitzers. The hereterogeneous defense groups, *Manassas,* the two navy gunboats, the two state gunboats, and six of the River Defense Fleet, dropped down to a point upstream from the forts and made ready for action. *Tuscarora* had burned up accidentally in January, so she was not there.

### III

There was a violent storm of wind and rain on April 10 and 11, which caused the water to rise so high in the swamps that the nuisance from rebel snipers was much abated. Porter, who had spent much of his time with the surveying parties, took three of his schooners up on Wednesday the 16th to try the range, while Farragut's gunboats covered them. It was found that the Confederates had cut away the vegetation across the point to the range of Fort Jackson's casemate guns, but the trees along the bank below gave cover, and the schooners were sweated into line along the righthand shore, their masts decorated with branches. The seamen of Farragut's fleet called their people "bummers."

Fire was opened on the 18th, Good Friday, from a

range of 2850 yards against Jackson, while one division of the mortars was taken across the stream to fire on St. Philip from 3700 yards. Porter rowed from one schooner to another to watch how the foundations of the mortars were standing up, while the woods shook and turned black under the shock and debris of their firing, one shot every ten minutes from each. The foundations held all right, but a little after noon a heavy shot went through the leader of the line on the east bank and she had to be shifted downstream.

About five, flames became visible above Fort Jackson. Shortly afterward dusk began to fall and Porter ordered secure for crews completely exhausted by manhandling the heavy shells, while he had himself pulled up in a boat and discovered that the fire had destroyed Jackson's barracks and citadel. (What he did not know was that five parapet and two water battery guns were disabled and nearly all the casemates damaged.)

This was a good beginning. The mortars opened again at six the next morning, while some of the gunboats moved up to engage with flat trajectory fire. The reply of the forts was rather surprisingly vigorous in view of the damage they must have taken. *Oneida* was hit and a solid shot went through and through one of the schooners, sending her to the bottom. By evening it was quite evident that Porter's boast of reducing the works in 48 hours would not be made good. He ordered night firing, one shell from each schooner every 30 minutes; and the tracery of fire through the dark soon told him that he was getting too many air bursts, so he had the fuses cut longer. That night a deserter swam off from Jackson and said things were pretty bad inside, parapets broken, casemates caved in and flooded, and the men demoralized.

Next morning, Easter Sunday, the crash of the mortars continued, while Farragut held a council of captains. The ammunition supply situation was far from good; he wanted to dash past the forts with the big ships. Practically all of them were against him, and Alden of *Richmond* finally produced a long memo from Porter, in which that officer protested that running upstream would leave a huge unreduced force in the fleet's rear and the mortars exposed to counterattack.

Farragut answered the strategic objection by saying that once the fleet was at New Orleans, Butler's troops could be brought through the bayous, and all other objections by saying he "would abide the result—conquer or be conquered." Captain Bell was ordered to take two of the gunboats up that night and break the barrier. Afterward the flag officer sat down and wrote Welles a letter of a character to make that correct man of business tear his wig:

I am not half supplied with anything. My shells, fuzes, cylinder cloth and yarn to make cylinders are all out. I asked for the shells I wanted and other ordnance stores and am told my demand is out of the question. I have not a solid shot on my ship and none in the squadron except a few on board the *Richmond*. We have only a few grape and canister; the fuzes of sufficient length were fired away the first day.

It was midnight when Bell slipped upstream with *Itasca* and *Pinola*. Almost everything went wrong; the detonating mechanism that was to have set off a huge charge of powder aboard one of the hulks failed to work, *Itasca* drifted ashore, and the Confederates spotted the two little ships in the dark, so that enough guns to crush them opened up. But Porter quieted down the guns with a quickstep barrage from his mortars, the chains were released from one of the hulks, *Itasca* was dragged loose, and there was a hole in the barrier. The rebels reacted by sending a huge fire raft through the gap at two-thirty in the morning. The flames reached as high as *Hartford's* mastheads; two of the gunboats collided trying to avoid it and both drifted into *Mississippi,* but no serious damage was done and Farragut had a useful warning on enemy techniques.

Next morning there was a strong wind blowing downstream. Farragut had fully determined to chance the passage, but did not wish to meet this competition, and so waited for another day, while the mortars growled on. That day the Confederates towed *Louisiana* down to a position just above St. Philip, with her guns in working order, mightily cheering the men in the forts, who expected the ironclad to go below and drive off the mortars, which were giving them a very bad time. It was possible to remount many of the guns knocked from their places, but the area of the forts was so cut up that they could not fire accurately; all the bedding had been burned; and there was little food or rest.

On the 22nd the wind still held. General Duncan tried to have *Louisiana* towed below the forts to attack the mortars, but Commodore Mitchell refused, having discovered that her guns could not be elevated enough to reach the Federal ships from any safe range, while a single mortar shell dropping on her unarmored upper deck would go right through and sink her.

On April 23 it fell calm and warm; Porter came aboard the flag to make one last protest about trying to take the fleet through. "Look here, David," said the old man. "We'll demonstrate the practical value of mortar work." He turned: "Mr. Osbon, get two small flags, a white one and a red one, and go to the mizzen topmasthead and watch the shells fall. If inside the fort, wave the red flag. If outside, wave the white one."

A tally-man kept count; the outsides won it in a landslide election. Farragut said calmly: "There's the score. I guess we'll go up the river tonight," and called his gig to row through the fleet and visit every vessel. To all he was as cheerful and confident as ever, but when Osbon expressed an opinion that not more than a hundred men would be lost, he said: "I wish I could think so." Hammocks were piped down and the crews told they might sleep till midnight.

## IV

At the stroke of two, with everything manned and shipshape, two red lanterns were hoisted to *Hartford's* mizzen peak, signal to get under way. The order of sailing was that Bailey in *Cayuga* led the first division, followed by *Pensacola, Mississippi, Oneida, Varuna, Katahdin, Kineo,* and *Wissahickon.* He was to edge rightward, close under St. Philip, and not fire his port guns. Behind him came Farragut with the heavy center division, *Hartford, Brooklyn,* and *Richmond,* who were not to fire to starboard; followed by Bell leading the light sloops and gunboats *Sciota, Iroquois, Kennebec, Pinola, Itasca, Winona.* Porter's armed ferryboats crept up the western shore to keep a detached water battery of Fort Jackson under smothering fire.

As the shelling of the mortars died away, the Confederates ashore lighted great piles of cordwood along the banks; and when *Cayuga* and *Pensacola* pushed through the torn barrier into that rushing light just at three-forty, the forts woke up, and simultaneously the mortars began their music again at redoubled speed. "It was as if the artillery of Heaven were playing on earth," Farragut reported later, and the whole scene was so swiftly filled with drifting smoke that the gunners in the forts were firing at flashes from the ships rather than the ships themselves. Into this pandemonium of gunnery came floating giant Confederate fire rafts, propelled by tugs.

Bailey and his division crowded close under St. Philip, and *Pensacola* and *Mississippi* put so heavy a fire of grape into it that the gunners were driven from their pieces and the gunboats following got through practically without damage except from the immobile and invulnerable *Louisiana,* moored above. They were already engaged with the Confederate ships by the time *Hartford,* with *Richmond* close behind, broke through the barrier and took on Jackson, howitzers in the tops firing at the barbette guns; the broadside pieces engaged the casemates. *Brooklyn* got involved with the barrier, swung cross-stream, took a bad pounding from St. Philip and a few shots from *Louisiana,* set Confederate *Warrior* afire with a broadside, and in the dark and smoke again crossed the river to find herself under the guns of Jackson. At this moment the ram *Manassas* lunged into the melee, firing her Cyclops gun into the big sloop and then ramming her ineffectually against the improvised chain mail. At the same time *Hartford* above the St. Philip water battery ran her nose into the bank dodging a fire raft. Another was pushed against her; she began to blaze along the port side, halfway to the tops. Someone heard Farragut say: "Oh, my God, is it to end this way?" But he recovered in a second and shouted: "Don't flinch from that fire, boys! There's a hotter fire than that waiting for those who do not do their duty! Give that rascally tug a shot!"

They gave her a shot and another, while Osbon rolled

into the fire raft three 20-pounder shells which blew it apart as it drifted clear, and suddenly, amazingly, the forts were passed; they were through. The first haze of dawn was in the sky and the Union ships upstream engaged with the Confederate fleets in a tangle so incoherent that it is impossible to give the details any order. *Varuna,* a notably fast vessel, got ahead of the rest and sent *General Quitman* into the bank aflame; was herself attacked by *Governor Moore,* whose Captain Beverly Kennon, though he had already lost a third of his crew to the fire of at least three Union ships, fired his big gun through his own bow into *Varuna,* then rammed her into the bank, where she went down. In turn *Governor Moore* was destroyed by a broadside from *Pensacola. Cayuga* fought a singlehanded battle with the River Defense Fleet, and every time she fired her 11-inch Dahlgren hit one of them, usually fatally. All six were soon ashore, afire and abandoned by their crews who, to tell the truth, did very little fighting. *Defiance,* indeed, did none at all; her captain was drunk and set her afire before she drew a shot.

*McRae* got into an action with *Iroquois* and had the worst of it; she was run ashore, crippled and sinking. Just as this happened *Manassas* came back upstream in the gray growing light; *Pinola, Richmond, Pensacola,* and *Wissahickon* all fired at her, and she took damage, but drove on, trying to rescue *McRae.* It was light enough for Farragut to signal *Mississippi* to run her down. The paddle-wheeler missed when the ram turned sharply, but the big guns did what ramming would not, and *Manassas* charged into the bank, her armor pierced, her engines smashed, the ship burning.

It was morning and all over. Farragut ordered the ships to anchor, wash down, and take count. *Varuna* had been sunk and three more of the 90-day gunboats were missing from the tally, all the ships were more or less damaged, and there were 37 dead and 149 wounded to report; but the forts were passed, the Confederate river fleet wiped out, except for immobile *Louisiana* and *Stonewall Jackson,* which got away upstream for a few miles, but in such shape that she had to be beached and burned.

Down below, Porter knew only that *Kennebec* had become entangled with the barrier and was unable to get through, *Itasca* drifted down with a shot in her boiler, and *Winona* had returned, cut to pieces with many casualties. But under the gray, grim dawn burning and battered wrecks now began to drift downstream, and they were all river ships with walking beams, Confederate rams, which gave reason for more than hope.

In New Orleans, the old city of the crescent, there was no such feeling. Just as the papers reached the streets in the morning with "GLORIOUS NEWS FROM THE FORTS," the alarm bells began to peal, the schools were closed, and the Home Guard fell in in the streets, not cheerfully. All afternoon and nearly all night drays rattled over the cobbles, carrying cotton from the presses to be fired on the quays, past women who cried openly. Crowds roamed about dangerously, looking for objects of anger. A night of shouting and bitterness at last gave place to day and showed the guttersnipes of the town rifling whatever on the waterfront was not in flames. The sound of guns came through the smoke as the Union fleet engaged and crushed in a few minutes the batteries of 32-pounders at the Chalmette, Andrew Jackson's old victorious battlefield, and now the masts of the Union ships were visible from the doomed city.

Ah, me! I can see them now as they come slowly around Slaughterhouse Point into full view, silent, grim, and terrible; black with men, heavy with deadly portent; the long-vanished stars and stripes flying against the frowning sky. Oh, for the *Mississippi!* the *Mississippi!* Just then she came down upon them. But how? Drifting helplessly, a mass of flames. The crowds on the levee howled and screamed with rage. The swarming decks answered never a word; but one old tar on the *Hartford,* standing with lanyard in hand beside a great pivot-gun, so plain to view that you could see him smile, silently patted its big black breech and blandly grinned. And now the rain came down in sheets.

The men in the forts mutinied and they had to surrender at discretion after a couple of days, while *Louisiana* was blown up where she lay. New Orleans was gone. Had France lost Paris or England, London? Napoleon III recoiled at once from diplomatic recognition of the Confederacy and Lord John Russell from pressing his fellow members of the British Cabinet on the subject. From this date forth Jefferson Davis' government rested on the sufferance of what its armies could accomplish.

. . . Afterward there was a tremendous amount of recrimination in the Confederacy about the reasons for not towing unfinished *Mississippi* to some safe hideaway upstream. A Congressional investigating committee developed the fact that Commodore Whittle did not know of any safe place upstream in view of the fact that Federal ironclads might be coming down any minute; and also that tugs could only move her at four knots, about the speed of the river at that season. She had no guns aboard and Farragut's gunboats could make eight knots.

# 5

## Assembly of Forces

As soon as he had received the surrender of Island No. 10, Foote steamed downriver with his gunboats to Fort Pillow, now become a very formidable fortress, since it had received whatever cannon from Columbus Polk had not been able to get to the Island. On April 13 some of the mortar rafts arrived and began to lob shells into Pillow from Plum Point Bend above, but at almost the same date General Pope received a call from Halleck to bring his troops to Pittsburg Landing for a concentration against Corinth, and there were left to support the river navy only two regiments, 1500 men.

This placed the Yankee admiral in a position he felt parlous. His damaged foot had not healed, he could only walk on crutches and was sick all the time; with no prospect of accomplishment he asked for relief and shore duty. Welles granted his old schoolfellow's wish, at the same time asking Congress for a vote of thanks, which would automatically enitle Foote to promotion. On April 23 Captain Charles Henry Davis was sent out for a few weeks of acclimatization as flag officer prospective. He was a Boston Brahmin and a great intellectual who had written two books and served on all sorts of planning commissions, including those which outlined the brilliantly successful attacks on Hatteras and Port Royal, "a most charming and lovable man" with gray rim whiskers. All the same it was too bad that the team of Grant and Foote had to be broken up; the others were made of different chemicals.

Davis agreed with Foote that nothing real could be accomplished against Pillow on its heights without army cooperation, so they set up a system of harassment, with one mortar raft always at Plum Point Bend, throwing a shell every half hour into the fort; a single gunboat on guard against Confederate surprise; and the remainder around the next bend, ready to step into action if the rebel river fleet, of unknown force and intentions, should come up to attack. Not long after Davis' arrival the situation was no little eased by the news of Farragut at New Orleans and the most dangerous of the enemy ships destroyed.

On May 7 Davis took over formally; Captain Phelps helped Foote to the deck, where he made a farewell address and was carried away with tears on his cheeks. He never did recover from the wound and died a year later in Washington, while on a desk assignment.

Two days after this, Montgomery called a council of war of his River Defense Fleet captains, and they decided to go up next morning to "cut out the mortars." They started about seven, eight gunboat-rams, *General Bragg, General Price, General Van Dorn, Colonel Lovell, General Beauregard, Sumter, Little Rebel, Jeff Thompson,* carry-

ing troops from General Jeff Thompson's Missouri command as artillerists and sharpshooters. *Mortar No. 10* was
stationed around the bend that day, with Stembel's *Cincinnati* as the duty gunboat, moored just behind the mortar to some trees at the bank, steam down and men holy-
stoning the decks since it was Saturday, the rest of the fleet
being five miles upstream.

The first warning the Union ships had was when *Cincinnati* sighted the onrushing rams only eight miles away.
She slipped her cables and drifted out into the stream,
with the engineers throwing oil and anything else inflam-
mable into her furnaces for quick steam, while the mortar tried to shorten range enough to hit one of them.
*General Bragg* came on at the head of the attackers with
a ten-foot bone in her teeth; she took the four 32's of
*Cincinnati's* broadside and crashed into her, a glancing
blow as the ironclad swung round, but one that tore a
6-by-12-foot hole. *Cincinnati* gave *Bragg* another broadside
that sent her drifting downstream with a list and her tiller
ropes shot away.

At this moment *Sumter* rammed *Cincinnati* in the fan-
tail hard, destroying her steering gear and letting in a rush
of water. Right behind came *Colonel Lovell;* the ironclad
got one shot into her, but she gave *Cincinnati* another telling buffet on the port beam and one of her sharpshooters
put a bullet through Captain Stembel's mouth. The ironclad rolled and went down, in water shallow enough to
leave her pilothouse above the stream.

It was a day so still and hazy that *Cincinnati's* signal
flags announcing the coming of the rebels had not been
seen, but the sound of guns told the story, and by this
time the rest of the Union ironclads were scrambling into
action, headed by Kilty's *Mound City. Van Dorn* met her

almost head-on with a blow that holed Kilty's craft so badly she had to be run into the bank, where she too sank.

But that was the end of the hurrah; *Benton* was in action now, and shells from her 9-inch Dahlgrens warned the Confederates that it was time to go home, while a shot from *Carondelet* went through the steam chest of one of the rams and sent her drifting after *Bragg*. There was no pursuit; as Davis pointed out, any damaged Union vessel would have drifted under the Fort Pillow batteries and there was not a ship in the fleet with power enough to tow a captured craft up against the current.

## II

So the Confederates had a quick victory, and after this Davis stationed two gunboats with steam up to guard the mortars, also placing more of them on firing duty to provide the greater annoyance. The chief effect of Plum Point Bend, however, was in another area of thought. In February of this year an elderly civil engineer with long hair named Charles Ellet, Jr., wrote a pamphlet demonstrating that a ship struck fairly by a fast ram must inevitably be sunk, and that in narrow waters it would be impossible to avoid rams. He sent copies of it to the War Department. On March 8 Confederate *Virginia* proved his point in Hampton Roads by sinking the sloop *Cumberland*. At this point the War Department was no longer lazy Cameron, but the dynamic Stanton; he promptly sent for Ellet, gave him a colonel's commission, and told him to purchase and equip any number of vessels that would be necessary to demolish the Confederate fleet on the Mississippi.

Ellet bought eight ships at Pittsburgh and Cincinnati,

four side-wheelers, four stern-wheelers, and had them altered in a manner to take advantage of mv². His first
thought was of something the Confederate ram-builders
hardly considered at all—having his ships deliver a heavy
blow without themselves being disabled. The bows were
packed solid with timber; down the centers of the ships
he built three longitudinal bulkheads, 12 to 16 inches
thick, strongly trussed to the sides with iron rods and screw
bolts. This made a rigid unit, capable of delivering the
impact of the whole mass at a single stroke. Boiler, engines,
everything that might be susceptible to shock, were
strongly braced in; to keep down weight there were no
guns whatever. He wanted 15-knot ships; probably the best
he could get could not make above 12; but even this was
far better than the fastest of the Confederate craft, with
their weight of iron and cannon. The crews were rivermen, not sworn into service; and by an act of high-level
nepotism all the commanders were Ellets, brothers, neph-
ews, and sons.

The news of Plum Point Bend brought a snowstorm of
telegrams from Stanton to Ellet about hurrying up, and
on May 25 the new commander joined the fleet as skipper
of the army ram *Switzerland,* with four of the others following behind. Ellet's orders required him to have the
"concurrence" of the senior naval officer present, and he
at once sought concurrence for a project of running his
wooden lancers past Fort Pillow for an attack on the Confederate river fleet. Davis did not approve, but he "con-
curred"; on June 4 Lieutenant Colonel A. W. Ellet of the
ram *Monarch* crossed the wooded point opposite Pillow
to spy out the ground. What he saw through his glass
convinced him that the place was being abandoned; he

hurried back to rouse his brother from rest at two o'clock in the morning, to ask permission to go downstream in a yawl and make certain.

He was perfectly right. The advance of the combined forces of Grant, Buell, and Pope under Halleck had become so menacing that Beauregard had given up Corinth without a fight three days before, and Pillow was outflanked as Columbus had been. The track was now clear to Memphis; rams and ironclads dropped downstream to a point not far above that city and anchored for the night, *Benton, St. Louis, Cairo, Carondelet* in line abreast across the stream, the rams *Queen of the West* (now the senior Ellet's flag), *Monarch, Switzerland, Lancaster* at the bank behind.

In Memphis there was some confusion but more confidence; the rams had beaten the Federal ironclads at Plum Point. In April, when Island No. 10 fell, *Arkansas* had been structurally complete and armored up to the main deck; she was taken down the Mississippi and then up the Yazoo, to where a new navy yard was established near Yazoo City. The armor for *Tennessee* was still somewhere on the Arkansas side of the river, and though her frame was complete, she was in no shape to be moved and would have to take her chances at Memphis. On the night of June 5 Montgomery held another council of war with his captains, and all agreed that the right thing was to go up and fight the Federals; but the officers of Jeff Thompson's Missouri troops did not assent, so they went on strike and marched off the ships. The matter was referred to General Beauregard by telegraph; in the morning he issued an order making Thompson and Montgomery jointly responsible for the defense of the river. Thompson in turn issued one detailing two companies of artillery for the defense of the ships; but before these men could reach them the morning of June 6 had come, the rams were already out in the stream, moving up as Davis' fleet came down. The Confederates knew nothing about the Ellet rams, which had been seen but taken for some kind of transport. Word of the impending action had run through the city like a current; thousands crowded to the bluff to see the Confederate victory, the women with parasols and Negro boys carrying wine and lunches in baskets.

Just at sunrise Ellet brought *Queen of the West* into the bank for a conference with Davis, when there came the sound of a gun from around the point, a mile distant. He cast off and started downstream, where the ironclads were already firing at the advancing Confederates; a curtain of smoke lay on the water, so that only the tops of funnels were visible. *Queen of the West* dashed through this pall, with Colonel Ellet on her hurricane deck, waving his hat and wildly cheered by the gunboats as his ship went past. *Colonel Lovell,* the center of the enemy line, came toward her, head and head, but at the last moment thought better of it and swerved; the fast *Queen* struck her midships, cut her in two, and sent her to the bottom in a matter of minutes. At one end of the line *Monarch* struck for *Price* and was in turn charged by that ship and *Beauregard.* The Union vessel was too fast, she slipped between them as they closed, *Beauregard* hit *Price,* tearing her port wheel off and sending her crippled ashore. *Monarch* came round in a graceful curve and rammed *Beauregard;* at the same moment a shell from one of the gunboats took out the latter's steam drum, and the Confederates waved surrender from her deck.

*Little Rebel* now had a shot in her machinery and was staggering into the Arkansas bank; *Jeff Thompson* was on fire. *Sumter* and *Bragg* maintained the fight for a while by backing water; but they could not take the 8-inch shells of the gunboats long and were soon also on the bank with their colors down. *Van Dorn* fled, the only survivor; *Lancaster* and *Monarch* chased her for several miles, but could not catch up.

The crowds on the bluff went home in tears after witnessing one of the briefest, most intense and decisive naval battles in history, less than 20 minutes. *Tennessee* had been fired on her slip when the Confederates saw they were not going to get anywhere; she and *Jeff Thompson* burned out, while *Beauregard* and *Lovell* were under water and past repair. The other four captures were patched up and became part of the Union river navy. The cost to their side was insignificant, but it included Colonel Ellet, hit in the knee by a pistol ball, a wound which should not have been fatal but seems to have run into blood poisoning. One of his sons landed in Memphis and hoisted the old flag over the post office.

In a sense it was the rams' victory, Plum Point reversed thanks to surprise reversed. The speed of the Ellet rams made it certain that the Confederates could not escape by running, though it may be doubted whether Montgomery's ships would have stood up any better against all those guns than the similar craft did at New Orleans. That is, Secretary Mallory had been at least half-right, and the kind of ships was very important; but his designers did not give him quite the right kind, nor his builders build them fast enough, nor his rivermen handle them with the skill of the Union captains. Port Hudson and Vicksburg were now the last bars to an open Mississippi and the way against them was open from both directions. Davis moved downstream.

### III

In March of 1862 General S. R. Curtis, who never did anything else of importance in the Civil War, defeated the Confederates so badly at Pea Ridge that it was said afterward that the entire state of Montana was populated by the rebel fugitives. He cut into Arkansas and in May asked for naval support and communications up the White River. Stanton passed the message to Welles, who said it would be given, and again passed to Davis, telling him to "use every effort" to supply the army in that quarter.

The original plan was for two gunboats and three Ellet rams, but the senior Ellet, still alive at that date, wanted an independent command and Davis refused him. Thus it became *Mound City,* the flag under Commander A. H. Kilty, *St. Louis, Lexington,* and *Conestoga,* with two transports carrying the 46th Indiana. On June 17 the expedition ran into enemy pickets; the troops were landed and the ships moved up to clear the stream, where Lieutenant John W. Dunnington, CSN, had sunk the Hollins gunboat *Maurepas* and two transports to make a blockade, and placed their guns on the bluff ashore.

There were only 114 men to handle these batteries, but Kilty did not know this, nor the positions of the guns. He refused Colonel G. N. Fitch of the Indiana regiment permission to encircle by land until he had tried naval fire. It was a mistake; quite early in the game a shot from a rifled 42-pounder pierced the front of *Mound City's* casemate and went right through the steam drum. There was a fightful explosion; the men in the casemate were cooked alive and those who got away overboard were killed in the water by Confederate sharpshooters, so that only 25 of 175 in the crew answered roll call next morning. The survivors went wild and plundered the ship, including the effects of the dying. Kilty himself was among the most severely scalded and his life was despaired of until July 21, when he got out of bed and recovered without warning.

*Conestoga* took the helpless ironclad in tow for downstream, while Colonel Fitch signaled the other ships to cease fire, and carried the batteries at the bayonet, capturing all left alive. One of them was Captain Joseph Fry, who was shot by the Spaniards in the '70's, while leading a filibustering expedition to Cuba. General Grant tried sending *Lexington* and *Conestoga* up the White again on June 28, but the water had fallen too low for them to get through, and transports could not operate without gunboat protection against guerrillas and light artillery.

## IV

As soon as the forts surrendered and Butler's troops were in control of New Orleans, Farragut sent Captain Bailey home with the captured battle flags and dispatches announcing his victory, and began to consider the question of what next. His first impulse was to use the heavy ships for an attack on Mobile, while the gunboats moved up to support an attack on Vicksburg; and in furtherance of this plan he sent Porter to Ship Island with his mortars. But nearly all the ships were badly in need of repair, there were no mechanics, and he was faced with the usual shortage of coal; so he decided to explore the river situation first. In the last days of April, Craven's *Brooklyn* was sent up to take Baton Rouge, with three gunboats under S. Philips Lee, which were to go on to Vicksburg.

Craven was one of those senior captains who had been the subject of Porter's remarks to Fox, an officer who always referred to Farragut as "the little man." Now he decided for himself that there was no use in taking Baton Rouge without troops to hold it, and ran on up to a point 20 miles below Natchez, where the machinery of *Itasca* and *Sciota* broke down and his coal got so low that he dared not go farther. There three more gunboats found him with changed orders: not to take his big sloop above Baton Rouge, she might go aground.

All seven ships turned downstream and were presently joined by *Iroquois, Hartford, Richmond,* and another gunboat. On May 9 the Stars and Stripes were hoisted at Baton Rouge under their guns, and Commander Lee was dispatched with five gunboats to take Natchez, followed by *Brooklyn,* an operation which Craven described as "a wild-goose chase." The other heavy ships followed, but *Hartford* got aground and had to take all her guns and stores out before she could be released, so it was May 16 before Farragut reached Natchez.

There he found that Lee and six gunboats had already gone on to Vicksburg, with 1400 troops under General Thomas Williams. Lee presently sent back a report that the guns at the town were mounted on bluffs 200 feet high and would have to be approached by the ships in single file, line ahead, because of the river's configuration; General Williams said that the rebels had five times his number of troops in the place and nothing could be done against it until the batteries were knocked out. An order to cut out the Confederate gunboats lying at the city was impossible of execution.

This apparent lack of fighting spirit so exercised the Flag Officer that he got on a gunboat and went up to discover for himself that it was all perfectly true. He brought the big ships up as far as four miles below Vicksburg and called a council of war. It was now May 24; the Confed-

erates had been strengthening their batteries, and all captains were agreed that the highest could not be reached
by guns from the river, though they might by Porter's
mortars. These were accordingly sent for, but before they
arrived, the mail from the Department came in, and it
was of a character to send the excitable Farragut into one
of his most spectacular tantrums.

A long letter from Fox said they had advices that the
fleet had ascended to Natchez, then returned to New
Orleans. This had greatly disturbed Lincoln. "It is of
paramount importance that you go up and clear the river
with the utmost expedition. Mobile, Pensacola and, in fact,
the whole coast sinks into insignificance compared with
this." The Confederate rams at Memphis might beat Davis
and cause the loss of Cairo and St. Louis.

Farragut could hardly know that behind this missive
lay a tangle due to Bailey. That captain with his flags and
dispatches was warmly received in Washington, told his
story to Welles, Fox, and Lincoln, and then on the floor
of the Senate. Grimes of the Naval Committee had just
introduced a resolution to both Farragut and the captain
who had brought his dispatches, when there arrived a
note from the super-correct Welles, who had in the meanwhile examined the dispatches. The note said there was an
"important discrepancy" between Bailey's account of passing the forts and Farragut's, and that any Senate action
should be withheld until the resolution of the problem.
As a matter of fact this important discrepancy was only
that Farragut or Farragut's clerk had failed to indicate
on the accompanying diagram that Bailey had led the line
in *Cayuga,* something the captain himself by no means
failed to mention. But the Welles note was enough to stop
Senate action and send Bailey back to the Department a

thoroughly disgruntled man. There he was questioned again, and the conversation turned to the upriver campaign.

Fox said: "How many ships has the Flag Officer sent to take the upper river?"

"None," said Bailey shortly. (It was true when he left.)

Fox: "Impossible! Sending the fleet up to meet Commodore Davis was the most important part of the whole expedition. The instructions were positive."

Bailey: "I believe he has forgotten them."

Hence Fox' letter of anguish to Farragut. Some of the edge was taken off (for Fox) by a missive which presently arrived from his friend Porter:

I never expect to hear of Farragut again. I have an idea he will ground on the bars of the Mississippi, and remain there the rest of the season. He went up without good pilots in those large ships where gunboats was all he wanted. He went up at a high stage of the river, and if the water falls he is done for and you can make up your mind to fit out a new squadron. If you can get one without having an old fogy in it, what a blessing it will be to the country. When I think of what a splendid thing we had of it here I collapse.

All the same Farragut had Fox' letter to answer. The Flag Officer pointed out his difficulties about repairs and coal; how hard it was to carry supplies upstream from New Orleans; that the time of half his men was out and they wanted to go home; his ships being fired on from Grand Gulf, Baton Rouge, and the banks along the stream; how he was losing anchors daily, without replacement. The big sloops would surely go aground if they were kept till the time of falling water and the gunboats would be unable to resist the rebel armored ram building upstream. "The elements of destruction to the Navy in this river are beyond anything I ever encountered. Why cannot the Department send us a monitor? It would be most gratefully received, as worth all the gunboats on the river."

Having offered this apologia, Farragut borrowed 3000 troops from Butler's command and prepared to run the Vicksburg batteries. It was the only thing he could do in view of the very positive orders from Washington, though the achievement promised him no such strategic success as at New Orleans, where the presence of the ships above the forts automatically cut off their supply and made surrender inevitable. On June 25 he was at anchor seven miles below Vicksburg, with *Brooklyn, Richmond,* 16 mortar schooners recalled from the Gulf, and four gunboats, of which *Itasca* had been badly holed by a surprise new battery at Grand Gulf while coming up. The mortars went to work at once; their fuses were defective and it took two days for them to get the range; but when they did, at two in the morning of June 28, the ships began to move upstream, *Richmond* leading because her chase guns were the best situate for fire at high angles. *Hartford, Brooklyn,* followed; then the light sloops and gunboats *Iroquois, Oneida, Wissahickon, Sciota, Winona, Pinola, Kennebec, Katahdin.*

The mortars opened at four, the ships were in action soon after, and the tops of the hills began to blaze. This was not New Orleans; smoke and dark quickly became so dense that the ships' gunners had to fire at flash, and Captain Bell noted that the most intense shelling was falling on slopes where there was no rebel artillery, while the upper batteries were not being reached. All the ships were hit repeatedly, and Farragut had a narrow escape when a shell went through the mizzen rigging just after he had been coaxed down from a post there. But by six in the morning they were through and splicing the main brace behind the long point of land the Mississippi makes by swinging a hairpin curve just above Vicksburg. The squadron had 15 killed and 30 wounded.

There they met Colonel Alfred Ellet and four of his steam rams. The fleets from river and Gulf were united and Farragut felt he had demonstrated he could pass forts whenever he pleased.

# 6

# The Ram Arkansas

Bᴜᴛ ᴡʜᴇɴ ꜰᴀʀʀᴀɢᴜᴛ counted noses above the fortress, *Brooklyn, Kennebec,* and *Katahdin* were missing. That the gunboats should fail to get through was no surprise; but the absence of the big sloop caused him to send a message of anxiety across the point of land to Craven: "I hope your ship has not been disabled and that your casualties have not been great, but I am most anxious to hear the worst."

Craven's reply was that the towing ships for Porter's mortars got in his way, the mortars themselves stopped firing at the wrong moment, and the batteries were raking him; he had been hulled twice but had no casualties. The summer heat on the Mississippi had become nearly intolerable; Farragut saw his ships melting down under damage and his men under dysentery, malaria, and the attacks of insects; this lack of resolution brought from him a curt note, demanding a full report. It came and it said that Farragut had told Craven the evening before the passage that he had not intended to leave behind any unsilenced batteries. This capped matters; in the first place, it was not true. Farragut's reply set him straight on the point of fact and then:

Now, sir, did you ever reach the bend of the river? I can answer for it that you were never within a mile and a half of it. I trusted to our early education "that no man did wrong who got his ship alongside the enemy," and that every man would follow his file leader, believing that all would do likewise, and no one regrets more deeply than I that you did not.

Now it was Craven's turn to lose his temper; he boiled back that: "No officer possessing the least particle of self-respect" could receive such a letter "without degrading himself to the level of a serf," asked for immediate relief, and got it. Bell was given the ship and Porter recorded his pleasure over the departure.

That same day Colonel A. W. Ellet asked permission to take *Monarch* and *Lancaster* (the latter commanded by C. R. Ellet, 19 years old) up the Yazoo for a look at the ram known to be under construction, as well as to see what else might be seen. There was no advance information; they might meet torpedoes, batteries, or naval vessels.

As a matter of fact, the river held *Polk* and *Livingston* of Hollins' fleet, and *General Van Dorn*, the last survivor of Montgomery's. The rams had only sharpshooters and a couple of boat howitzers apiece, but their appearance so excited the Confederates that they burned all three of their ships. The Ellets surveyed the wrecks with satisfaction, were halted by a raft barrier, and steamed back down

to the Mississippi after one of the cheapest naval victories
of record.

At the turn they found Davis had arrived with *Benton,
Carondelet, Cincinnati,* and *Louisville,* curious-looking objects in the eyes of the ocean navy. A great round of salut-
ing and visits was going on. With Porter's mortars growl-
ing intermittently in the distance, the two fleet commanders agreed that gunboats could not scale hills, and
since there were no troops to do so, very little could be
accomplished beyond blockading Vicksburg. Meanwhile
the increasing menace of Confederate mobile artillery on
the banks of the lower river came up, with the rifle snipers
who helped the guns, making it necessary to give supply
vessels gunboat convoy; also the necessity of soon taking
the big sloops downstream, since the water was falling
dangerously. Porter groused about not getting a fair allow-
ance of provisions for his mortar men; and Farragut con-
sented to board *Benton* for a trip down to the batteries to
see how modern war was fought. They got into range; a
shell came through a port and strewed fragments of dis-
mantled humanity around the deck.

"Dammit!" cried Farragut. "I must go out on deck. I
feel as though I were shut up in an iron pot, and I can't
stand it!" He never did achieve confidence in the river
gunboats.

A dispatch arrived from Secretary Welles; General
McClellan's campaign on the James was going badly and
12 of Porter's mortars were to be sent 2000 miles to help
him at once, a proceeding which Farragut quite reasonably
thought strange. On his way down Porter wrote Fox a
gloomy letter about the quantities of lead, beef, bacon, and
flour being brought down the Red River and so across the

Mississippi by the rebels; but there was nothing to stop that either until the army appeared in strength. The fact was developing that an amphibious operation requires both elements, neither wholly valid without the other.

It thus became a case of marking time; and on the morning of July 15 *Carondelet* was sent into the Yazoo with *Tyler* and *Queen of the West* to see about that ram.

## II

On May 26, 1862, Lieutenant Isaac N. Brown, CSN, who had had such bad luck with *Eastport* on the Tennessee, received orders to assume command of *Arkansas,* "and finish the vessel without regard to expenditure of men or money." He found her at Greenwood, in shape to have discouraged an Eads: the guns were lying on her deck without their carriages, only one blacksmith forge and five carpenters were working, and the barge that had brought iron for her armor was foundered in the Yazoo. There was no crew.

Brown went to work like a rat in a maze. In two days he had moved the ship down to Yazoo City, hired 20 blacksmiths from neighboring plantations and 200 carpenters from the army to work on her in day-and-night shifts, raised the armor barge, and converted the hoisting engine of a river steamer to drive a system of mechanical drills for the ironwork.

He wanted *Polk, Livingston,* and *Van Dorn* to be kept downstream with steam constantly up, ready for any Federal intrusion. But Commander Pinkney, in temporary charge of the station until Captain William F. Lynch could arrive from Richmond as Hollins' relief in charge of all forces on western waters, would not consent to this arrangement. When some of the dangerous Federal gunboats were reported coming upstream, the three ships were unable to move, so they were burned.

The crew Brown worked up consisted of men from the burned gunboats, with 60 volunteers from Jeff Thompson's command, who felt a little badly about the way their companions had let down the Montgomery flotilla. The ram was intended to be chocolate brown, but the paint was bad, and mostly she was red with rust. When Lynch did arrive from Richmond, he could do no more than express his disappointment; *Arkansas* was "very inferior to the *Merrimac* in every particular. The iron with which she is covered is worn and indifferent, taken from a railroad track, and poorly secured to the vessel." How he would have improved matters or how they could be improved, he did not say.

Brown drove right past him to the completion of the ship, for the rivers were falling and delay might be fatal. There was no time to bend the iron armor around the curve of the quarter and stern, so boiler iron was loosely tacked over these parts "for appearance' sake." As to other matters Brown bypassed Lynch to deal directly with General Van Dorn, in command of the area.

Earl Van Dorn remained an incurable optimist down to the moment he was caught in bed with another man's wife and had his brains blown out; he advised Brown that there were 37 Union ships in the river upstream from Vicksburg, but that a craft of *Arkansas'* force could easily run through them, refit under the batteries; "then, ho! for New Orleans!"

This chimed perfectly with Brown's own ardent and bellicose ideas; he turned down an offer from Captain Lynch to accompany him, and, weighing anchor on July 14 with a ship more or less complete, steamed down the

Yazoo. That afternoon, at the mouth of the Sunflower River, it was discovered that steam from the imperfect engines, which had a habit of stopping dead-center, had penetrated the magazine and wet all the powder. Brown had the stuff landed and dried on tarpaulins in the sun-struck area around an old sawmill, and at daylight of the 15th cast off to proceed. It was his intention to have attacked the Federal ships while they were having breakfast, to which he understood their people were greatly addicted. But the ram got aground and it was full light when Brown saw ahead three enemy ships coming upstream in line abreast, *Carondelet* in the center. The Confederate captain made his men a brief speech, ending: "Go to your guns!" "Many of the men had stripped off their shirts and were bare to the waists, with handkerchiefs bound round their heads, and some of the officers had removed their coats and stood in their undershirts." Brown ordered no fire from the bow guns for the moment lest it diminish speed, and charged in to try his ram against *Carondelet*.

The startling appearance of the ram around the bend, full-armed and ready for action, threw everything in the Union squadron into sixes and sevens, with each commander acting on his own. Lieutenant Joseph Ford of *Queen of the West* at once perceived that his frail craft, with the current canceling her speed advantage, would stand no chance against the ram; he turned and frankly ran. Walke of *Carondelet* and Gwin of *Tyler* made independent but identical command decisions; to fire their bow guns (which missed), then swing round and fight the stern pieces downstream, expecting the racket to rouse out the rest of the fleet.

As it happened, this was a bad decision. The faster *Queen of the West* and *Tyler* kept well ahead, but *Caron-*

*delet* could not, and every time *Arkansas* fired, her shells went right into the unarmored stern. *Cardonelet's* own projectiles caromed off the armor without doing damage except to take off the head of an Irishman who stuck it out of a port to see how the battle was going. At the point where Yazoo joins Mississippi, *Carondelet's* steering gear was shot away and she went into the bank, badly damaged, with 20 casualties, steam coming out of her ports and men jumping overboard. *Arkansas* turned on *Tyler,* whose skipper was swearing furiously because *Queen of the West,* instead of swinging round to attack the ram from astern as he had signaled, was tearing downstream with smoke pouring from her funnels, hailing the fleet to tell them what had happened.

They were fairly caught napping. Not a ship had steam up or guns loaded. The firing had been heard indeed, but everybody thought it was the gunboats having an affair with some batteries, and even when *Tyler* appeared, hard hit, with eight killed and 17 wounded, the first comment was: "There comes the *Tyler* with a prize." Now the drums rolled quarters and the decks swarmed with men casting loose pieces as the ram came upon them.

The temperature in *Arkansas'* engine room had reached 130 degrees, and details from the gun crews were relieving the exhausted firemen, but she had thus far sustained no damage except by a shot from *Tyler,* which broke in the pilothouse to kill one man and wound another. Brown noted that the Union rams were anchored behind the intervals between the bigger ships, and ordered *Arkansas* held close to their line to keep the Ellet ships from working up speed.

The day was without wind; as the rebel ram opened the ball by firing her bow guns at *Hartford* and her broadside into *Kineo*, smoke settled so thick that both sides were soon shooting at flash. Shot rang against the ram's side "as fast as sledgehammer blows" and one of them, probably from *Richmond*, came through to lay 16 men on the deck. A rifle bolt knocked out 11 more; the funnel was so perforated that *Arkansas'* speed dropped to a bare knot above that of the current and she was unable to ram *Benton* when that ship loomed through the smoke to starboard. But *Lancaster*, which had succeeded in getting out to prepare a ramming blow, was disabled by a shot through her boiler, and the rebel ram drifted and steamed down under the Vicksburg batteries, to be received with cheers soon silenced by the sight of the carnage on her gundeck. General Van Dorn, who had not partaken of the sight, wanted her to go back up at once and "sink six or eight of the Federals"; Brown said no.

Farragut was furious.

You may imagine [wrote Davis] his excitement at this scene of mortification and rebel triumph. He desired to make it worse by putting his whole command in all sorts of perilous positions, and treated my reasons as very cold and repulsive.

The old man, in fact, was all for charging right down under the forts and attacking the ram forthwith; if not prevented, she would obviously go downstream to smash up *Brooklyn* and the mortars remaining there. After a while the staff got Farragut calmed down enough to postpone the move until preparations could be made, the guns loaded with solid, *Hartford's* heaviest anchor hoisted to her main-yardarm to be dropped on the ram's deck, and the river ironclads readied to furnish cover by an attack on the batteries, while *Sumter* accompanied the ocean ships to run the enemy down.

It was already growing dark when the start was made and misty night had settled as the ships reached Vicksburg. Brown had anticipated the attack and shifted position under the twilight when his move would not be observed. In the murk the red ram under a red bank was quite invisible until they were right upon her, and Farragut's ships could only fire one broadside each at the flash of her guns as they went past. *Hartford* did succeeed in putting an 11-inch through *Arkansas'* armor, but *Winona* and *Sumter* were both badly hit in return and it was a failure.

The next day came in hot, with rain and squalls of wind. Farragut wrote Davis a letter of vehemence and anxiety: let both fleets together go to Vicksburg in broad daylight and fight it out with that ram and the batteries. In reply Davis counseled patience, prudence, self-control. "I have watched eight rams for a month, and now find it no hard task to watch one." (Neither of them could know that at that moment Porter was telling friend Fox that Davis was a little too patient, prudent, and self-controlled for the rough work of the river command.) However, Davis did consent to confer with the ocean officer across the point on July 21, hottest day of the year. The result was they agreed that next morning an attempt should be made on *Arkansas* by Dirty Bill Porter's *Essex* (whose skipper thought her shot-proof), with *Queen of the West,* which A. W. Ellet had volunteered. Davis' ships would cover the upper batteries, Farragut's the lower, while *Sumter* came upstream to join the ramming.

Aboard *Arkansas,* Brown had trouble getting men to fill out the crew, since General Van Dorn would allow only volunteers to go, and when mortar shells began dropping round the ship, the new surgeon cried: "Oh, Louisa and the babes!" and hid in his stateroom. When the two

Union ships came downstream at earliest dawn, just as Farragut's fleet was getting under way, Brown saw through the game at once, slacked off his bowline and presented only his sharp armored prow for ramming, while he engaged with the guns. It was about a ten-shot battle; one of *Essex'* heavy shells broke through the Confederate's armor to knock out 14 men; in return she took a hit in the engines, which proved she was by no means shot-proof, and went drifting down to join Farragut. *Queen of the West* got in only a glancing blow and moved back upstream, much torn by shot, but nobody hurt. *Sumter* never got into action at all for reasons which her commander, Lieutenant Henry Erben, was unable to explain.

That was the end, draw by perpetual check. Farragut could see no point in staying that far upstream, where he could accomplish nothing, the water was falling and he had many sick; and Davis no point in staying that far down. The two fleets sparked apart like particles carrying identical charges, Farragut to New Orleans, Davis to Helena, Arkansas, now in Union hands. *Sumter* and *Essex* went with Farragut, their engines being insufficient to take them back through the batteries. Mr. Secretary Welles thought the whole business "the most disreputable naval affair of the war" and wrote Farragut a letter in which he said: "It is an absolute necessity that the neglect or apparent neglect of the squadron should be wiped out by the destruction of the *Arkansas*." *Essex* and two of the 90-day gunboats were left at Baton Rouge; the rest went below for repairs and assignment to Gulf blockade duty.

As for *Arkansas*, she remained at Vicksburg, repairing damages. It was hard to find carpenters, but all hands were mighty cheerful. An answer had been found at last to the pullulating numbers of Federal ships, the line of communication across the Mississippi was restored, the attack had been beaten off, and Vicksburg was secure.

## III

General Earl Van Dorn, burning to take advantage of the upswing, now decided to retake Baton Rouge and relieve the blockade of the lower river. A land force under General Breckinridge was dispatched against the place and he asked the cooperation of *Arkansas*. The request went (as was perfectly proper) to Commodore Lynch, as naval officer in charge of the area. Lynch (as was also perfectly proper) said certainly, and ordered the ram downstream, without informing himself that her engines were giving a great deal of trouble or that Captain Brown was ashore, in bed with a fever, assured that nothing important would happen until he and ship were mutually repaired.

*Arkansas* cast off then, on the morning of August 3, with Lieutenant Henry K. Stevens in command, and moved downstream. At the mouth of the Red River the engines became so cranky that Stevens called a council of war. Decision: the ship would press on. The next morning at daylight they heard the sound of Breckinridge's guns as he attacked, and mingled with them the deeper boom of the Federal naval artillery—from *Essex, Kineo,* and *Katahdin*—firing in support of their troops. Accompanied by the Hollins gunboat *Webb* and a new one named *Music, Arkansas* hurried toward the scene. At the bend above the reach that leads to Baton Rouge, while Stevens and the pilot were agreeing that they would first ram *Essex* and then take on the gunboats, the starboard engine gave out suddenly and the ship ran hard and fast into the bank.

Breckinridge sent an officer to say he could press on no farther in the face of the naval guns, but would attack again as soon as the Federal ships were driven off. The engineers worked all day with files and chisels. At dusk the ironclad began to move, cheered by ladies who waved handkerchiefs from the shore, but she had gone no more than a hundred yards when the crankpin in the rocking shaft of the starboard engine broke square through the middle. They set up a forge on the gundeck and made a new one, finished by dawn, when *Essex* was observed coming upstream, two knots against the current. The new crankpin was hastily installed and *Arkansas* steamed out to meet her, Stevens' plan being to run a little upstream to gain distance, then charge down with the momentum of the current behind him.

At this precise moment the port engine gave way and *Arkansas* again steamed into the bank, in a position where only one gun bore, with *Essex* coming up astern and opening fire. It was hopeless; Stevens himself lit fires in the cabin and wardroom and, with tears running down his cheeks, ordered all hands ashore. The ram's active career had lasted 23 days.

*Essex* fired at her as she drifted burning downstream, and Bill Porter claimed all the credit in a letter direct to Welles, in which he blamed the failure to destroy the ram at Vicksburg on Farragut and Davis, at the same time abusing the army for not closing that fortress from the rear. He was well called "Dirty Bill"; his brother David had had nothing to do with him for 15 years, and never would again. When Welles found out the facts of the engagement, he set it down in his diary that: "Like all the Porters, he is a courageous, daring, troublesome, reckless officer."

All the same Mallory's bright prospects had been destroyed; Captain Lynch was out of a job because there was no longer any Confederate navy on the Mississippi. On August 9 Farragut had the news that Congress had created the grade of Rear Admiral for the first time in American history and that he was its first recipient. He could now take a 15-gun salute and go back to the Gulf, satisfied that he had come too strong and too soon to be countered by the Confederate efforts, however valiant, however pertinacious. As for them, their trouble really goes back to the fact that many men of many minds were trying to be individuals without coordinating with the rest; but perhaps this was inevitable in a state founded on the right of the parts to separate from each other unless each had its way.

# 7

# The New Deal
# and Vicksburg: Act II

WITH THE SPRINGING APART of the Union fleets and the
destruction of *Arkansas*, the pace changes completely. It
was equilibrium; neither side any longer had the means
for a naval offensive or an amphibious one. The Confederacy could send food items and arms brought from
Europe through Mexico and Texas down the Arkansas
and thence East, and it did so: with difficulties, but they
were mechanical and not military, the supplies moved.
Port Hudson, at the southern end of their river control
area, had become very strong, and passing it would be a
major effort. Union ships between that place and Vicksburg, would have to get supplies somehow, which was
confoundedly difficult, quite aside from the barriers offered
by the big forts to unarmed vessels. From Vicksburg down,

the rebels fell into the habit of firing a few rifles or a field gun from a town or plantation at anything that moved. The Union policy was conciliation; it was assumed they would not retaliate.

The change seems to have begun just after the attack on Baton Rouge. When Farragut heard of it, he started upstream with two of the big sloops, transports following. As he anchored just beyond Donaldsonville, there was the noise of firing from downstream, and the news was that the transports had been attacked from the town. On the way back to New Orleans, the admiral ordered the Donaldsonville mayor to get the women and children out of town and burned the place.

Sometimes these raiding affairs became quite serious. In July, while Farragut was still at Vicksburg, the supply bark *Houghton* started upstream with provisions and ordnance stores, plus $100,000 in gold for the fleet's payroll. She was armed with 4 32's in broadside and an 11-inch Rodman forward; her motive power was an oldish river steamer which broke down and forced her to tie up at the bank. Next morning an old Negro signaled from the shore; being contacted, he said his master was a rebel colonel, who had gathered all the men in the neighborhood to the number of several hundred, and they would drift down in barges and bateaux that night in the dark of the moon to board and capture the supply ship, of whose value they were perfectly aware.

The tale was confirmed by the crosstree watch, who saw the enemy gathering beyond the point. It was past midnight when the ship was cleared for action, guns loaded with grape and canister; cutlass, boarding pike, and revolver issued to each of the crew. The dog watch was out when the click of oars was heard; peering through the dark *Houghton's* crew made out the Confederates, divided into groups for simultaneous attack from both beams. As the rebel yell rose from them, the battle lanterns were lighted and all the guns let go.

I am an old man now; I have been often in battles since then [wrote one of the Union sailors 23 years later], but never yet have heard of anything to equal the yell of agony that broke the stillness of that night. Five of the bateaux were blown to fragments. In the remaining boats, about a hundred men still unhurt made a dash for us, and five of the boats succeeded in grappling to the lanyards of our standing rigging, when that clear voice rang out: "All hands repel boarders!" The next five minutes witnessed a perfect fusillade of musketry, mingled with the clash of cutlass and saber, the rebel yell, and the cheers of our men as the last of the attacking party leaped from our deck to reach the last boat. Only four gained a foothold on our deck and three of them now lay there dead.

The Confederates could have learned from Horatio, Lord Nelson, that a boat attack which fails is the most costly of all naval enterprises. They seemed to have learned it from somewhere, because there is no record of their trying that trick again.

The news that followed Farragut from New Orleans was that Lieutenant Henry Erben had run the gunboat *Sumter* into a bank, abandoned her, and set her on fire. "Depend upon it," wrote the old man, "that this feeling of timidity or prudence, as they are pleased to term it, must be suppressed," then bade New Orleans farewell and sent his big ships for the much-needed repairs. He was supposed to blockade the coast from Pensacola to the Rio Grande, and lacked means for the task, beside having had trouble at Galveston; the supply of coal was always utterly inadequate, and so was that of fresh provision.

As soon as the Admiral was out of the river, Butler ordered the troops out of Baton Rouge; the ships went with them; and equilibrium descended a few miles farther.

Davis behaved much as Farragut, though he did not have the other's exterior responsibilities. Early in August a new reconnaissance up the White River showed that it had fallen so far that gunboats could not get in. Later in the month *Benton, Mound City,* and *General Bragg* with four of the Ellet rams were sent downstream under the general command of Lieutenant Commander S. L. Phelps to thumb a nose at Vicksburg. They captured a big transport at Milliken's Bend, then went up the Yazoo to where a river barrier stopped them, taking and burning a fairish quantity of stores on the way, but were unable to obtain any solid information about the new ram the rebels were supposed to be building at Yazoo City. Negro contrabands were so vague and contradictory that Davis assumed there was no present danger, established *Benton* and *Carondelet* as duty ships at Helena, and sent all the rest to Cairo for repairs, much worn from ramming and the shock of firing guns from green-timber hulls.

He was content to wait for events and an army ashore that could cooperate with him. "More of a scholar than a sailor," Welles set him down. "Has gentlemanly instincts and scholarly acquirements, is an intelligent, but not an energetic, driving, fighting officer, such as is wanted for rough work on the Mississippi," a judgment that doubtless reflected Fox' transmission of Porter's views. The Secretary's great navy bill had gone through Congress July 16, giving him pretty general powers of reorganization and ending the anomalous situation by which the navy furnished designers, guns, ammunition, officers, and men for river work, yet all under army authority. October 1 was set as the date for the transfer of all ships except the Ellet rams to Navy control, but in September Fox wrote to Davis that the whole squadron was to "assimilate to the Navy in rank, pay, &c., &c.," rear admirals ranking with major generals, so the thing was an accomplished fact before the target date.

Meanwhile in that no-progress summer of Second Bull Run and Perryville, Mr. Welles had been meditating, and in September he acted. David Dixon Porter was summoned from Newport, where he was just getting over a bad bout of intermittent fever, he supposed for a wigging over his treatment of Farragut. Mr. Welles calmly told him that he, Porter, was to be sent as acting rear admiral in charge of the navy on western waters; how soon could he leave. It was one of the most amazing promotions in naval history, for Porter was only a junior commander, thus moved up to lead the nation's largest fleet—only possible because of the new law and the state of flux into which the war had thrown all ranks. Porter simply accepted it as his due and said he would leave at once.

Welles' reasons went into the famous diary:

He has stirring and positive qualities, is fertile in resources, has great energy, excessive and sometimes not over-scrupulous ambition, is impressed with and boastful of his own powers, given to exaggeration in relation to himself—a Porter infirmity—is not generous to older and superior officers, but is kind and patronizing to favorites who are juniors. It is a question, with his mixture of good and bad traits, how he will succeed. His selection will be unsatisfactory to many, but his field of operation is peculiar, and a young and active officer is required.

Porter willingly agreed to cooperate with the new army that General McClernand was raising in the West to take Vicksburg; Davis was politely moved upstairs to the Bureau of Navigation, or personnel office, where his qualities could be of real use.

The new admiral set out on his trip west in October, while Grant was maneuvering obscurely from Memphis toward the rear of Vicksburg. His first stopover was Pittsburgh, where he talked to ironmongers and other suppliers of materials, and told them that his demands would be greatly increased; so must their work staffs. He found it annoying that although armor iron had to be rolled and guns cast there, no ships of importance could be built because everything had to be shipped across tenacious bars.

At Cincinnati, Porter inspected the new ships under construction. There were two powerful single-turret monitors, with heavy guns and 12-foot draft, *Catawba* and *Tippecanoe,* now barely up to the lower deck and certainly not to be finished in another year; the new admiral approved them.

There was also a class of ironclads of different size but similar construction, building by a contractor named Joseph Brown to the design of Samuel Hartt, apparently to demonstrate his originality—*Chillicothe, Indianola, Tuscumbia.* They were intended to get rid of the objections to the Pook turtles by having a casemate forward, containing 2 11-inch rifles (three in *Tuscumbia*) working on pivots so they could fire through ports over the bows, abeam, or at an angle aft. A casemate astern between the humps enclosing the paddle-wheels carried 2 9-inch for stern fire; they had flat decks and the armor was three inches. *Indianola* and *Tuscumbia* also had twin screws between the wheels and an extra set of engines to drive

Rear Admiral Porter's flotilla arriving below Vicksburg on the night of April 16, 1863. In the foreground General W. T. Sherman going in a yawl to the flagship *Benton*

The Confederate ram *Arkansas* running through the Union fleet at Vicksburg, July 15, 1862

The *Pensacola* disabling the *Governor Moore*

The *De Kalb,* formerly the *St. Louis* (type of the *Carondelet, Cincinnati, Louisville, Mound City, Cairo,* and *Pittsburgh*). From a photograph.

The *Carondelet* running the Confederate batteries at Island Number Ten (April 4, 1862). After a sketch by Rear Admiral Walke.

The Battle of Memphis (June 6, 1862), looking south. After a drawing by Rear Admiral Walke. (Left to right: *Carondelet, Benton, St. Louis, Cairo, Louisville, Queen of the West, Monarch.* In the distance Confederate fleet advancing.)

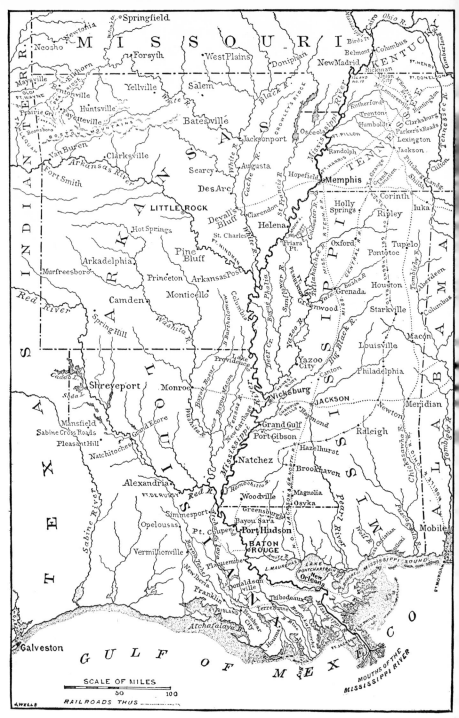

Campaigns of the Mississippi Valley

The mortar boats at Island Number Ten

MAP OF
## KENTUCKY AND TENNESSEE

SCALE OF STATUTE MILES
10   30   50   100

The *Brooklyn* attacked by the Confederate ram *Manassas*

Jas. B. Eads

Colonel Charles Ellet, Jr.

Confederate sharpshooters and swamp hunters attacking mortar boats

Rear Admiral Henry Walke

D. G. Farragut

Bird's-eye view of the passage of the forts below New Orleans, April 24, 1862. The Second Division in action, 4:15 A.M.

them. It was an interesting idea but almost everything was wrong with them. *Chillicothe's* gunports had been cut five inches too high and her sides patched to fit, while her pilothouse was located so far forward that she could not be steered while the guns were firing. All were so badly put together that *Tuscumbia's* deck fell down six inches the first time she fired her guns, and her armor was held to the woodwork by bolts less than four inches long. The woodwork itself gaped and shrank. Both in this ship and *Indianola* the central engines took up so much space that there were no quarters for the crew.

The builder blamed all the troubles for these ships on Hartt's miserable designs and the inability to get money from the Navy Department, while Hartt took it out on the wretched construction. Porter thought the armor utterly inadequate and his efforts to get things amended ran into the superintendent of construction in the West, one Captain J. B. Hull, a member of the old seniors' club and an amiable man, but an expert in red tape, who informed Porter that no "apartments" to house the crews on the ships could be added until he had gone through channels to the Department and secured official approval.

The temporary rear admiral thus departed Cincinnati under a cloud of fury almost as black as his beard; but when he reached Mound City and St. Louis, he began to find conditions notably better. The former place was become a vast floating city, with even barge quarters for Negro stevedores; at the Carondelet, Jim Eads was busy again.

In April of that year, 1862, a telegram from Welles called the great builder to Washington, where in view of reports of Confederate armor on the Mississippi, he was asked for designs for two armored gunboats of very light draft. The classic battle of *Monitor* and *Virginia* was not a month old; Eads borrowed a drawing board in Chief Constructor Lenthall's office and on the spot turned out a design for a single-turreted monitor, turtle-backed up from a freeboard of practically nil, with a turret of Eads' own design, working on ballbearing instead of the central spindle of the Ericsson system, and port shutters that closed automatically as the guns recoiled.

Fox shook his head when he saw the drawings, and said that the draft would have to be under six feet because of water levels in subsidiary streams; also that the Ericsson turret had given full satisfaction and there was no use interfering with a going concern. The ultimate result was three river monitors, *Osage, Neosho,* and *Ozark,* under construction when Porter arrived, five-foot draft, with Ericsson turrets and 2 11-inch rifles each; they were proof against anything but the heaviest guns.

After Eads left for St. Louis to build them, it occurred to Welles that his ideas might not be so bad after all; they had turned out notably juicy in the case of the river ironclads. He recalled the builder by another telegram and asked for a second design, this time a double-turret monitor. Eads' new design embodied his own peculiar turrets (which, incidentally, were to become the standard type in future years); and though Welles expressed a certain degree of peevishness over this insistence on ballbearing turrets, he ended by giving Eads a contract for four more monitors, *Chickasaw, Kickapoo, Milwaukee,* and *Winnebago,* each with two turrets, one Ericsson, one Eads, carrying 4 11-inch and being turtle-backed like the smaller ships. They were to be screw-propelled; the little monitors had stern wheels in humps.

In June, Davis had written to Welles on the heels of the

White River expedition, reinforcing what had been learned from the "timberclads" at Pittsburg Landing and Shiloh. He wanted a number of "boats of small draft to maintain control of the tributaries of the Mississippi during the dry season." Other officers reinforced his request; half a dozen purchases were made in August by the amiable Captain Hull and Porter found them being plated with boiler-iron under the direction of Samuel Hartt.

Their skins would keep out musket balls; most of them mounted 6 24-pound howitzers and could carry a contingent of sharpshooters behind their iron; best of all their draft was only 22 inches.[1] Porter was delighted with him; they fitted exactly into the pattern of aggressive war he intended to make. He demanded many more ships and set the yards at Pittsburgh, Mound City, and Cincinnati so hard at work on them that he had 22 completing by the end of the year, with more to follow.

He was also happy with two new ironclads, *Lafayette* and *Choctaw*, even though they were designed for conversion from heavy river steamers by his brother and unfriend, Dirty Bill, under what authority no one has ever been able to determine. In shape they were much like Pook turtles, with wheels inside the casemates, but rounded at the ends instead of having square corners and armored all over. *Choctaw* had 3 11-inch, *Lafayette* 2 11-inch forward; the former carried 2 30-pound rifles in broadside, the latter 4 9-inch—more powerful ships than the Eads craft. They would be ready during the winter, many of the tinclads at once, with the rest and the monitors fol-

[1] Technically "without load"; but most of the load was in the howitzers, which were removable if really shallow water was encountered. The specifications are general; individual ships differed a good deal.

lowing. Before spring the Union river navy would be able to apply a maximum of pressure on an enemy who had already lost his power of fighting afloat.

Porter went down to Mound City, broke out his starred admiral's flag aboard *Benton,* and changed the name of *St. Louis* to *Baron De Kalb,* since the navy already had a *St. Louis,* an oceangoing sloop.

The work of personnel reorganization on joining the navy was more complex; many men had been signed on by Army at higher rates of pay than Navy protocol allowed; these had to be dropped down to bring them in line with the oceangoing sailors. And many of them had to be hove out altogether and replaced with Negro contrabands, a job Porter had to do by himself in each individual case, since the institution of a naval staff was yet unknown. Four hundred sick had to be discharged and replaced, a hospital to be found and set in operation—so many things that the easygoing Davis had left undone. At Cairo, Porter did find that he had inherited Captain A. M. Pennock, a relative of Farragut and "a real trump"; he was sent downstream temporarily to take charge of operations between Helena and Vicksburg. Lieutenant K. R. Breese was brought from the mortar flotilla to be flag captain.

## II

The black-bearded Isaac Brown heard of the destruction of his beautiful ram while he was on his way to join her; he gathered up the crew and took them back to Vicksburg on wagons. With the Confederate Mississippi navy wiped out except for *Webb,* up the Red River, and *Ponchartrain,* up the Arkansas, there was not much to be done in the tactical area, so Brown expanded his shipyard facilities and began to build.

The command relationships with Van Dorn of the army remained somewhat ambiguous, since Mallory had practically abandoned any effort to control the Mississippi, but for the time being there was no violent pressure on the land front, and Brown seems to have possessed both persuasiveness and the ability to get along with most people. Van Dorn loaned carpenters and mechanics from the forces besides those Brown had used in the building of *Arkansas.* Five sawmills, a machine shop, a blacksmith's shop were set up at Yazoo City, and three ships were laid down, enough to keep all hands busy without getting in each other's way. One was a fast-screw gunboat to be named *Mobile,* an answer to the Ellet rams; one a duplicate of *Arkansas,* the ram *Republic;* the third a monster wheel-driven ironclad, somewhat on the lines of *Louisiana,* but even larger than that unhappy dragon, and of more original design. She was to have four wheels and two propellers and be the biggest warship ever built inland.

Brown expected to get the engines for the three from Richmond. It took so long to set up the shops and gather sufficient material, especially such items as timber and nails, that the year had turned and Earl Van Dorn's brains had been blown out by the justifiably jealous husband before the keels were laid down.

Meanwhile it was noted that the Federal gunboats were likely to come back up the Yazoo. Brown and his men took over the defense of the stream "rather by inference than by any direct orders." Two of his masters, named McDaniel and Ewing, were mechanics and knew something of explosives; they had heard of experiments with torpedoes in the east and offered to try to make some. Brown thought it a good idea and they began to improvise.

A five-gallon whisky demijohn was packed with powder

borrowed from the army and supplied with an artillery friction tube. This torpedo was placed in a wooden box, the whole suspended some feet below the surface on small iron wire and arranged to be exploded when a ship made contact with the wire. At the same time Brown got hold of a certain Dr. Fretwell, who in turn had connections with a businessman named Norman; they made improvements on the McDaniel-Ewing model to allow of explosion from rifle pits in the banks. Fretwell and Norman contracted to build 50 of the improved torpedoes, but never finished all of them because of the lack of wire, batteries, containers, etc. But at least the Yazoo had some torpedoes and a 6-inch gun mounted at Haines' Bluff to keep the damyankees from dredging them up. The army added more guns and some low-powered torpedoes of its own. An obstruction made of piles and railroad logs was placed in the river below the bluff.

This was the naval defense of Vicksburg and the Yazoo at the time action came. To understand this action it is necessary to comprehend what the Yazoo delta is. Just below Memphis the high bluffs that enclose the river retreat slightly eastward. Some 25 miles down the bluffs are pierced by a series of rivers which cut down through deep-etched gaps—Coldwater, Tallahatchie, Yallabusha— uniting to form the Yazoo, which turns to run nearly parallel to the Mississippi, assembling slow, winding items from the diamond-shaped area of deep-soiled lowland westward—Steele's Bayou, Sunflower, Little Sunflower— until Yazoo meets Mississippi, just above Vicksburg, where the bluffs slant southwest again to dominate the main stream. This is another set of Chickasaw Bluffs.

Yazoo City is at the foot of the bluffs, about halfway between Vicksburg and the mouth of the Tallahatchie. At

the Tallahatchie exit a not-inconsiderable work was erected
to keep Federal forces from working through the streams
from northward and getting into the high ground behind
Vicksburg. It was named Fort Pemberton, after the Penn-
sylvanian-gone-South who was placed in charge of the
area command when Van Dorn got himself shot.

## III

The opposing command was Grant, with the Army of
the Tennessee, based on Memphis. He started moving
down the high ground to get into the rear of Vicksburg
in November; found the roads very bad and logistic support inadequate. This led to a new concept—that of marching into central Mississippi as far as the Yallabusha to
draw Pemberton out of Vicksburg to face him, while
W. T. Sherman, his most trusted subordinate, went down
the river with the cooperation of the navy and sliced in
behind the fortress at Haines' Bluff of the Chickasaw Bluff
system. Reinforcements were promised Grant from new
levies now raising; Sherman would have the cooperation
of a large number of troops from Helena in the trans-
Mississippi Department.

Grant's interview with Porter lasted less than an hour;
it was no case of love at first sight, but each understood
precisely what was wanted by his opposite number and
was prepared to give it.

While I was looking earnestly at Grant, trying to find out
how much of a man there was under the plain exterior, Grant
was regarding me to see what amount of work there was under
the gilt buttons and gold lace with which the Department had
bedizened my coat.

The general said little, but set it down that he could rely

on the admiral's judgment and nerve to complete absolutely anything he chose to undertake.

Early in December then, Porter sent *Carondelet* (Walke),
*Cairo* (Selfridge), *Pittsburg* (Lieutenant Commander G. M.
Bache, a nephew of the admiral's), with the new tinclads
*Signal* (Lieutenant John Scott) and *Marmora* (Lieutenant
Robert Getty) down to the Yazoo to clear the way. Union
intelligence had a fairly good line on the ironclads building but knew nothing about the torpedoes until one
exploded near *Signal* when the two tinclads were sent
20 miles up the stream and sighted floats and buoys.
Lieutenant Scott told Walke (who was in general charge)
that he could clear out the torpedoes without difficulty
if he were given ironclad support; the Confederates had
rifle pits all along the eastern bank with light artillery
that made boat work virtually impossible and was a danger
to tinclads.

Selfridge, with the high forehead and well-brushed sideburns, requested to lead the expedition, and Walke sent
him in on December 12, *Signal* and *Marmora* running
ahead. Shrapnel from the ironclad rapidly drove out the
men in the rifle pits and everything was going well when
*Cairo* ran into one of Brown's demijohn torpedoes well
short of the heights. There was a violent explosion forward
and the ship sank in 12 minutes, not losing a man; but it
was the end of that show.

Porter heard the tale and the news of torpedoes in the
Yazoo when he came downstream in *Black Hawk* at the
head of all the ships he had been able to gather, and met
*Marmora* coming up with the survivors. Selfridge, full of
youthful dignity, conscious that he had tried to bull
through without getting all he should from the tinclads,
and with the albatross of his father's dismissal at the mouth

of the river hanging round his neck, stiffly asked for a court of inquiry.

"Court!" snapped Porter. "I have no time to order courts. I can't blame an officer who puts his ship close to the enemy. Is there any other vessel you would like to have?" He swung round to the flag captain without waiting for an answer. "Breese, make out Selfridge's orders to the *Conestoga.*" He had that kind of mind. It is likely that there was recorded in it the name of everyone who commanded anything under steam on the Mississippi, to the tune of some 200 vessels.

At Memphis, Porter found Sherman, surrounded by new recruits, confusion, and hurry, and told him about McClernand having some kind of deal with Washington that would give him an independent command with a good deal of rank; whatever they did together must be done quickly. Porter and Sherman hit things off at once, each agreeably surprised by the other's easy, offhand manner. They agreed that it would be a tough campaign and dependent upon exquisite timing. Not only was there the menace of McClernand and his vague important authority from upstream, but N. P. Banks, another political officer, who had replaced Ben Butler at New Orleans, was supposed to be taking Port Hudson before closing on the rear of Vicksburg. He would want to take over troops and ships as soon as he got there. In addition, it would be impossible to communicate with Grant across the Yazoo diamond. General and admiral would be an element of force at the end of the line of communications winding back by water to Memphis. Nevertheless, everyone was full of energy and confidence, the soldiers betting they would spend Christmas in Vicksburg.

Just below Haines' Bluff the Yazoo does a sinuous angle

to the west before joining the major stream. In this half-drowned angle, where no one was sure what was land and what morass, Sherman had to debark his troops for the assault on the bluffs. He began going ashore on Christmas Day; Porter sent Bill Gwin's *Benton* with some of the tinclads up to the point where Yazoo cuts loose from the bluffs to shell out the Confederates there and cover Sherman's left flank. (Walke was on his back with a bad dose of intermittent fever.) The tinclads cleared the torpedoes, but the channel was so narrow that only *Benton* could fire. She went into action on December 27 and did well against the batteries at the angle of Yazoo and bluffs, which contained 18 heavy guns, 7½-inch and up. Over 30 shot glanced from her armor, but three came through the ports, and Gwin, one of the most valuable officers in the squadron, was mortally wounded by a cannonball that took off his right breast and most of the arm. No priest could be found to give him the Extreme Unction his church desired.

*De Kalb* replaced *Benton* the next day and on December 29 Sherman made his assault on the bluffs. That night he came aboard *Black Hawk*, wet to the skin, muddy, and depressed; it had been a complete failure, all the Confederates were in the reception committee. Neither he nor Porter could know that a Confederate cavalry raid had burned out Grant's forward supply base, forcing him to retreat toward Memphis and leaving Pemberton's command time to get downstream and hold the bluffs against the element of force at the end of its winding line.

The next day arrived a message that General Mc-Clernand had reached Milliken's Bend and was assuming command of Sherman and all his men. He expected Porter to cooperate with him.

# 8

# Vicksburg, Third Act

PORTER HAD NEVER THOUGHT particularly well of West Point officers, and the impression was deepened by a fairly nasty incident at the Newport Club, the first night he was able to go out after his return ill from service with the mortars, when a batch of West Pointers snubbed him heavily. He was therefore predisposed to regard Mc-Clernand, the non-West Pointer, with favor. After that general and Sherman came aboard *Black Hawk* on January 7, 1863, it took about ten minutes to dissolve this sensation into one that McClernand was a pompous ass. He talked grandiosely and in general terms about what he was going to do, and how much Sherman had deteriorated army morale by not being polite to newspapermen; as to what specific strategic action he intended he expressed not the slightest idea. Certainly not against Vicks-

burg, which he had been specifically appointed to take—
it was "too big a boo."

Sherman suggested that there was something of a question of national morale involved; an army of well over
30,000 men had gone down to the Vicksburg region without doing anything at all. If Porter would detail Shirk
or Phelps, who had previously cooperated with the army,
he, Sherman, would be glad to undertake the reduction
of Fort Hindman at Arkansas Post, a few miles up the
Arkansas. This would at least bring more territory under
the old flag and hinder the Confederate ironclad building
at Little Rock. (Actually there was no such ironclad, but
this was the best information available at the time and
place.) McClernand loftily reminded Sherman that all he
commanded was a corps; all high-level decisions belonged
to the ranking officer. Sherman got up and walked out of
the cabin; Porter leaped to his feet in his nightshirt: "If
General Sherman goes in command of the army I will go
along with my whole force and make a sure thing of it.
Otherwise I will have nothing to do with the affair!"

After a couple more exchanges the pompous ass and the
two businessmen got down to details. They would start
next morning early, before reporters could give the show
away. Porter himself would be the naval head. He took
*Lexington* (Shirk), *Louisville* (Lieutenant Commander
E. K. Owen), *Baron De Kalb* (Lieutenant Commander
John G. Walker), and *Cincinnati* (Bache) as the support
force, each towed by one of McClernand's transports, since
the ironclads were, as usual, low on coal and could not
breast the current burning wood. There were also *Black
Hawk* (Breese) and the tinclads *Rattler* (Lieutenant Commander Watson Smith), *Signal, Romeo, Juliet, Glide,
Springfield, New Era,* and *Forest Rose.*

The route was up the White through gloomy swamps and by a connecting bayou to the Arkansas—a device to avoid too-early observation. On the night of January 9 the squadron tied up three miles below the fort and Mc-Clernand gave orders for the troops to land from the 50 transports that had followed the naval vessels. There was comparatively little dry ground and it was mostly close to the banks; three regiments were put on the west shore to move upstream and see that the Confederates did not get away by crossing the river.

Within the fort there was no intention of doing anything of the kind. The commander was J. W. Dunnington, who had the batteries on the White when *Mound City* was so fearfully mauled the previous March. It is indicative of the state of the CSN on the rivers that he had sent *Ponchartrain* up to Little Rock, brought down her crew to be gunners in the fort, and himself had been ranked into the army as colonel commanding the Third Brigade. His fort was a square work with bastions, covering the reaches above and below. It had 10 rifles and a 9-inch smoothbore; they were all casemated in thick oak plated with railroad iron to the thickness of one of the rams. Above the fort an obstruction of iron and piles barred the river; behind it fieldworks ran through gullies and woods, with fields of fire where cotton had grown to give protection in the rear. Range buoys had been set out between 1200 and 1000 yards downstream, from which point it was correct to assume that the enemy would fire, since their armored gunboats would be nearly proof at that range.

Next morning, a cloudy day and chilly, part of the Union troops began moving up the river bank, while Sherman took the rest by a detour to get behind the fort. At three in the afternoon McClernand rode down the bank to tell Porter that all was ready. The naval officer doubted this (as a matter of fact it was untrue and Sherman was stuck in the swamps) but, having observed the range buoys, ordered the ironclads in to 400 yards, *Lexington* followed; the tinclads to use their howitzers on the field-works.

The Confederates made good practice as the ships reached the range buoys and *De Kalb* had a number of casualties, but the enemy fire fell off rapidly as soon as the gunboats moved in close, and it was early evident that the ships would gain the upper hand, while *Lexington* and *Black Hawk* were deluging the trenches with shrapnel. Dark fell without any sign of the troops making an assault; Porter dropped back downstream to an obbligato of the screams of wounded horses and hammer and chisel ringing in the fort as its people made repairs.

Before the frosty dawn word came from Sherman that he was in position at last; Porter moved the ironclads into position again, 50 yards from the fort, sending *Rattler* above it to enfilade the trenches there, while he himself buzzed about in a tug. *Rattler* could not make it against the river obstruction and word came that McClernand's men were retreating, but the guns of the fort had fallen silent after an hour's firing, so Porter took *Black Hawk* in and boarded across the embrasures. White flags everywhere and a scene of devastation greeted him. The iron-plated casemates had been penetrated by the ships' artillery and every single gun was dismounted or smashed; the place was full of human corpses and those from an immense depot of artillery horses that had been kept within.

As the admiral was surveying the havoc there was a rafale of musketry fire from the rear trenches and then white flags began to appear there also. An adjutant came galloping through the lines to say that General Smith was coming to take possession and the naval people must clear out at once. Porter snapped: "We've put the rebels out of this place, and if you don't take care, we'll clear you out also!" At this moment Smith arrived in a swirl of cavalry; the adjutant told his story. "Will he, by God?" said the general. "Let me see him; bring the fellow here."

"I stepped forward and said, 'Here I am, sir, the admiral commanding this squadron.' At this announcement Smith laid his right hand on the holster of his pistol. I thought, of course, that he was about to shoot me, but instead the General hauled out a bottle and said: "Be God, Admiral, I'm glad to see you; let's take a drink!'"

This was A. J. Smith, who later gave Forrest such a beating at Tupelo. He was known as "Whisky" Smith; he and Porter became great friends and always worked closely together. Grant called the Fort Hindman expedition a "wild-goose chase," but the place was taken with 6500 prisoners, almost as many as at Island No. 10, and the Confederates burned all the ships they had up the Arkansas. The guns afloat did the job.

## II

By this date Grant had secured from Washington un-equivocal assertion of his authority over McClernand and McClernand's men, and brought the rest of his army downstream to camp opposite Vicksburg. It was the season of freshet; his men had to be strung out for 60 miles along the banks and there was very little they could do toward reaching the much-desired high ground around the city. Sherman was urging the strategically correct course of taking everything back to Memphis for a new overland campaign, but Grant had a lively sense of the tremulous state of national morale in that black January after Fredericksburg and Stone River, and refused to turn back. Meanwhile he employed his men on a project promoted from Washington—digging a canal across the point of land opposite Vicksburg, through which transports could be taken to land men below the fortress. It was a project doomed to failure, for the canal had to be opened at a point where there was no current force to scour it deep enough to carry ships and the lower batteries of the fortress commanded the exit anyway; but it kept the people busy and the newspaper correspondents amused, while Porter tried to find a naval solution.

The admiral had brought his provision ships, floating machine shops, hospitals, and stores to the mouth of the Yazoo and set up a mobile forward base there. His striking force consisted of the Pook turtles, the Ellet rams, *Indianola, Lafayette* (by no means complete as to men or guns), and *Chillicothe,* with seven tinclads. The remainder of the tinclads, as fast as complete, were being assigned to patrol beats along the Mississippi, Ohio, Cumberland, and Tennessee. A big steamer was seen unloading under the guns of Vicksburg; C. R. Ellet, the very young, offered to go down with *Queen of the West* and sink her, and on February 3 was given permission to start.

The permission came not from Army but from Porter; in November there had been a cloudy and wordy battle across the Cabinet table in Washington over the principle of unified command on the Mississippi. Stanton got angry, Welles won, and the Ellet rams were transferred to Navy orders, officers retaining their military titles, and the organization being called the Marine Brigade. It was recruited up to a regiment of infantry, a battery of artillery, and a regiment of cavalry, real horse marines, men and mounts being carried aboard the rams.

Ellet banked his ship with cotton bales to make her shot-proof, but on the way down it struck him that his wheel was badly placed for the rapid maneuvers he would have to make in ramming a ship under fire. He stopped to change it, and though dawn was already breaking grayly when the job was finished, he was ardent with youth and would not wait for the next night. The result was that the uppermost battery sighted him and fired alarm guns. By time he was abreast the city the works were all manned and shooting. The cotton kept out most of the solid shot, as intended; but after Ellet had driven once against the steamer, by no means a crushing blow, shells set fire to his cotton armor, all hands had to turn to to heave it overboard, and *Queen of the West* passed on downstream with her woodwork much torn and her primary mission unexecuted.

Ellet pushed on to Warrenton, which was on Grant's side of the river, repaired, took on stores, and moved down toward the mouth of the Red to see whether he could stop some of the trans-Mississippi traffic. Almost immediately he took three fine steamers carrying provisions to Port Hudson and came back to Warrenton to deliver them—a good beginning for the '63 campaign.

The height of the waters now offered new opportunities; all the complex of streams and bayous in the Yazoo diamond were brimming to a depth where they could carry steamboat traffic. In the old days the Mississippi had annually flooded through a gap called Yazoo Pass into the Coldwater and so to the Yazoo, but the Pass had been closed by a levee when the Southern Railroad was built. Why not, suggested someone, blow out the levee, send ships and troops through, and win a beachhead up the Tallahatchie on the high ground north of Vicksburg?

Porter approved and placed the expedition under Lieutenant Commander Watson Smith, who had done so well with *Rattler;* he had his own ship, the *Lioness* ram, the old *De Kalb* (Watson), the new *Chillicothe* (Lieutenant Commander J. P. Foster), the tinclads *Forest Rose* (Master George W. Brown), *Romeo* (Ensign Robert B. Smith), *Signal* (Lieutenant Cyrenius Dominy), *Petrel,* a mortar boat, and 800 troops under Brigadier General L. F. Ross.

The levee was broken on February 3, the day Ellet took *Queen of the West* downstream, and the river, nine feet above the level of the old pass, gushed in, bearing a tangle of dead trees and logs on its breast. It was four days before the water level became high enough for the ships to follow. In spite of the speed of the current, which was still filling the channel, the debris was so clinging, there was so much sawing to do in snubbing around sharp bends by means of hawsers, that progress was miserably slow. Overhead cypress and cottonwood formed arches, grown with wild grape that made a perpetual twilight. Grant's engineer, James H. Wilson, a young man not two years out of the Academy, with a Napoleonic goatee, was an immense help and understood perfectly that the thing must be done with relative speed and surprise if at all. He kept everyone up to the mark by his energy and cheerfulness and the men sang through four days of terrific toil, in spite of the fact that branches stripped the ships of everything exterior. *Petrel* lost her wheel and had to go back; both of *Romeo's* smokestacks were torn away; *Chillicothe* had her bottom stove in by a stump and it was kept in place by shoring from above.

On the 11th they reached the Clearwater and good

going to the Tallahatchie—and found a newly built fort with heavy guns. The obvious thing was to fight through; the two ironclads moored side by side, bows downstream, and opened fire, while the mortar fired over them from the rear. At this point there were two simultaneous unfavorable developments; *Chillicothe's* forward port shutters were jammed by shot and Watson Smith went insane, fainting and coming out of it to issue a series of orders in the most complete gibberish.

The two ironclads pulled out in response to one of these, but *Chillicothe* returned in the afternoon and proved how poor her construction was by having four killed and 15 wounded, mostly by bolts driven out of the armor to fly like bullets through the casemate. Next day the ironclads tried again; *Chillicothe* ran out of ammunition, and though *De Kalb* temporarily silenced the big guns in the work, there was no place to put Ross' men ashore for a land attack, and the artillery would clearly open again if the ironclads pulled back to let the transports run through. The military man said he could do nothing without siege guns. There were none; and after 13 days of sloshing around in the mire and caring for poor Smith, who had flashes of lucidity, but was even more broken down physically than mentally, the expedition dismally pulled back out. At the junction of Yazoo Pass and Mississippi it met some thousands of men Grant had dispatched on a rescue mission.

There had been uncomfortable rumors from upstream, but definite news of this failure did not reach Porter until the end of March. He sent Smith home and wrote Welles an indignant letter about the shortcomings of *Chillicothe's* construction—"I consider Mr. Hartt to blame. As a private individual I would not employ him in anything." The tone was acerb, which is not surprising, in view of the other tidings Porter had to report during that uncomfortable month.

First there was the matter of *Queen of the West*. On February 10 she captured a small steamer, armed it as a tender, then worked into the Atchalfaya on the flood waters, where on the 12th she destroyed a train of Confederate army wagons carrying beef, then went back up the Red. There the steamer *New Era* was taken, loaded with supplies, and her pilot was pressed to guide the ram up the river. This proved a mistake; he drove the ship hard aground right under a battery of 4 32-pound guns, whose shot tore through her sides as though they were paper. One of them carried away her steam line; Ellet could not burn his ship because he had an engineer aboard with a broken leg. Therefore everybody jumped overboard and began to float down on bales of cotton to where the tender picked them up. Just as she reached the place where the prize *New Era* was moored, the tender too ran hard aground, lost her rudder, and had to be destroyed.

Ellet knew *Webb* was some 60 miles upstream and would probably be after him and the survivors. He set all hands to work throwing overboard the corn with which *New Era* was loaded and worked downstream to the Mississippi under fog and rain, with no food aboard. All the next day *New Era* tried to steam up the Mississippi, but the only fuel was cypress, so water-soaked that it would barely give the ship steerageway for a knot an hour. Officers and hungry men were just discussing leaving her and taking to the woods when the lookout reported two enormous smokestacks standing through the fog. The smoke coming out was black, signifying a coal-burning ship, therefore a Union vessel.

It was in fact the new ironclad *Indianola* (Lieutenant Commander George Brown), sent through the Vicksburg batteries by night, with a coal barge lashed on either side, to reinforce *Queen of the West*. The news that the ram was certainly in the hands of the enemy put Brown in a bad position; he had only men enough to work two of his guns and no light artillery. He sent Ellet back overland to ask for another gunboat to come down and help him, then ran down to the mouth of the Red, but, lacking a pilot for that stream, turned back northward to meet the expected support, taking his coal barges along.

*Indianola* was in the area of Warrenton on February 24, nine-thirty of a coal-black night, when the lookout sighted ships coming upstream at considerable speed. They were in fact *Webb* (Captain Charles Pierce) and *Queen of the West* (Captain James McCloskey), the latter completely repaired and loaded with sharpshooters, with two cotton-clad steamers carrying troops for boarding, *Doctor Beatty* and *Grand Era,* the whole under command of Major J. L. Brent. *Indianola* turned to face them and opened fire with the 11-inch; missed, and before she could reload, was struck by *Webb. Indianola* swung to interpose one of the coal barges; the ram cut right through it and hit the ironclad's side, not a damaging blow. The coal barge began to sink, and as it went down *Queen of the West* struck nearly bow to bow, again without much damaging *Indianola,* but in the dark, with her inexperienced crew bothered by the fire of rifles and fieldpieces from the cotton-clads, the ironclad's guns missed again.

*Webb* and *Queen* each rammed again; the force of the former's blow swung the ironclad around and *Webb* dashed past upstream. This made her the greater danger, since it placed her off the ironclad's vulnerable stern and wheels;

Brown sent his men running aft through the gallery to the 9-inch. *Queen* struck again during the process, and this time the guns did not miss; the ram swung clear and upstream with two killed and 33 wounded. She was not crippled, however, and before the guns could be reloaded, *Webb* came charging in against the starboard wheelhouse aft, throwing men to the deck and putting the wheel completely out of business. Not two minutes later *Queen* struck *Indianola* squarely aft; the rudder went this time; the ship took a heavy list and began to go down by the stern, so her commander ran her into the bank and surrendered. The fact was that *Indianola* had been completely unsuited to her mission, without light or medium guns to make the Confederates keep their distance, and not even men enough for the guns she had.

Porter heard the heavy, slow firing from downstream and held the sound an evil omen, soon confirmed. He had an urgent project for getting up the Yazoo to set Grant on high ground, and had only five of the Pook turtles with him; sending any one of them downstream to clear up the situation was to risk what happened to *Indianola,* and he could not spare a squadron. He got off telegrams northward to hurry on the ironclads building and meanwhile conjured up a plan to make ingenuity substitute for means. The whole work force of the floating base was turned to on an old barge; she was built out with dummy paddle-wheels and up with sloping sides, through which projected a formidable-looking tier of wooden guns; there were two pork-barrel turrets atop. Amidships were placed a pair of funnels made of beef barrels, with a huge pot of tar and oakum at the base of each. A pilothouse was placed on the upper deck and dummy boats on dummy davits; then she was tarred all over, her "fires" were lighted and she was set adrift down-stream, bearing a sign DELUDED PEOPLE, CAVE IN.

Never was ruse better rewarded. The upper batteries sighted her early, and as she came abreast Vicksburg, all the guns opened fire. The heavy shot did not seem to affect her; the telegraph lines from the city grew hot with the news that a huge Union armored monitor was bearing downstream, so strongly protected that she needed neither the cover of her own fire nor any accompaniment of coal or cotton barges. *Queen* came up in the gray of dawn and sighted the monster for herself; it was all true, the Union giant was plowing along with her guns out. The ram passed the word to *Webb,* which was in no better shape than herself, both racked and leaking from the ramming of *Indianola.* They fled downstream with the other ships, losing *Doctor Beatty* in an accidental collision during the process. *Indianola's* 9-inch were hove into the stream, the 11-inch were destroyed by being fired muzzle to muzzle with slow-matches, and the ship blown up. The Confederate dominance of the central Mississippi had lasted just over 24 hours.

### III

In the meantime Porter in person had been trying to penetrate the high water through the bayous to reach the rear of Vicksburg. There is a branch called Steele's Bayou; it communicated with Cypress Bayou, then with Deer Creek which in turn, through another branch called Rolling Fork, reaches the upper Sunflower and thence the Yazoo, well above Haines' Bluff. The admiral started on March 14 with *Louisville* (Owen), *Cincinnati* (Bache), *Carondelet* (Murphy), *Mound City* (Byron Wilson), and *Pittsburg* (Hoel) with four tugs and a pair of mortar rafts for shelling. Sherman followed ashore with a corps of 10,000 troops.

It was a strange cruise; the ironclads steamed through a vast and virgin forest, so deeply drowned that there was everywhere 15 feet of water, close under trees where coons, rats, mice, and wildcats had taken refuge from the flood. An experiment by *Cincinnati* showed that big trees in the way could be knocked down by ramming, but this gave no help against clutching branches that tore at boats and smokestacks. The fleet was not yet a full day in when enormous piles of burning cotton appeared on either bank, and a darky watching them said the fire would go on for two days. Porter closed his ports and the ships ran through a choking murk of smoke and almost intolerable heat. Beyond, they came on a rough bull of an overseer, sitting quietly with his bare-breasted Negro mistress and a group of tan-colored children; he exchanged words of mutual disrespect with the admiral. By sunset only eight miles had been covered through a system so winding that four of the ships, 500 yards from each other, would be pointing in as many different directions.

Toward morning the sound of axes was heard; Porter sent a tug with a howitzer on ahead, heard her fire a couple of times, then saw her return to say she had found a large gang of Negroes being given whisky as they chopped down trees along the banks. One three-foot trunk was already across the channel, but it presented no great obstacle when a hawser had been attached, run through snatch-blocks, and the full power of an ironclad applied. By the second night there was hardly a whole boat in the squadron and skylights were broken everywhere by falling debris; the banks were high enough to march on, but there was no sign of Sherman.

The third day went the same; at morning of the fourth *Cincinnati* in the lead reached the head of Rolling Fork Pass, where there was a small collection of houses and a large one of Negroes, eager to join the "Linkum" gunboats but perfectly worthless as labor, since they knew nothing but hoeing cotton. Just beyond, a series of green patches swept right across the water—willow withes (the Negroes said) which would be cut and used for basketry when the bottom dried out. Porter sent a tug on ahead to test this obstacle; she got into the willow mess and could not move in either direction, *Cincinnati* at full speed tried to rescue her and stuck fast also; all hands turned out to try to clear the willows, and as they were about it there was a redoubled report and two shells, recognizably rifled Whitworths by their sound, burst near the ships.

This was a dilemma, since the banks were so high over the ships that the guns could not be elevated enough to reply. The mortars Porter had sensibly brought with him took care of things for the time being, but now there began to drift down against the upper end of the willow thicket vast numbers of logs, sent down by the Confederates to form an absolutely impassable barrier. At the same time the Whitworth battery opened from a new position and a contraband brought in word that 2000 men were marching cross-country to take the fleet in the rear.

About four in the afternoon the mortars drove the Confederate battery off for good. Porter carried hawsers from the tug and *Cincinnati* to two other ironclads astern, and with all backing hard, got his ships out of the willows after an hour's labor. But there was clearly now no going on and the element of surprise had been lost. Porter scribbled a note to Sherman, entrusted it to a stocky black who described himself as "the country telegraph," unshipped his rudders, and let the ironclads drift backward down the current. He was worried lest the rebels think of throwing enough cotton into Rolling Fork to form a dam and lower the water level on him while he was still in the woods. After dark the sides of the ironclads were greased to prevent boarding and a landing party was put ashore with the howitzers.

The next day the ships began to be bothered by sharpshooters, and soon the pat of their bullets was incessant, although they seemed to prefer the smokestacks as targets and very little damage was done. Presently the gunboats reached a place where eight large trees had been felled across the channel and the men could hardly go outside to clear them. But Porter turned his broadside guns into simulated mortars by firing them at maximum elevation with very reduced charges; not long later the Confederates on the banks could be seen running and Sherman had arrived.

By March 28 the squadron was back at the mouth of the Yazoo and every mechanic and carpenter in the floating base was busy with repairs. The only results of the expedition were that Sherman got a brace of very fine turkeys, and $300,000 worth of cotton came out on the decks of the ironclads, not enough to pay for the damage. Welles' comment was: "The accounts from Porter are not satisfactory. He is fertile in expedients, some of which are costly without adequate results." The diary does not mention the dummy ironclad.

# 9

# The Deadlock Broken

AFTER FARRAGUT TOOK the ocean ships to New Orleans, he faced outward, toward the Gulf and its blockade, where there were problems of the most serious order. The only real river ship he had was *Essex,* and she was hopeless against the current except through areas of slack water, while General Ben Butler had no troops to spare beyond those needed for holding down mutinous New Orleans. But in December the new strategy of concentrating on opening the Mississippi began to raise its head; on the 15th there arrived at New Orleans six transports with 20,000 men, a holograph letter from Lincoln and a new commander, General N. P. Banks. He was tall, handsome, and smooth-shaven (a marvel for those days), a former governor of Massachusetts and Speaker of the House, who had not done very well during the hard fighting in the East, but could perhaps be expected to win a much-desired reputation in a subsidiary theater and with navy help. People in the Crescent City called him "the dancing master"; he gave balls in hope of reconciling the population.

His orders said he was to take Port Hudson, move upstream to help Grant capture Vicksburg, cut the railroads in central Mississippi, take all the posts on the Red River, then the forts at Mobile Bay. "These orders," concluded old Ponderosus Halleck, who wrote them, "are not intended to tie your hands or to hamper your operations in the slightest degree." It was a not-inconsiderable budget of projects for 20,000 men; and though Banks did send a force upstream for the reoccupation of Baton Rouge with gunboat support soon after his arrival, he seemed more willing to set up a government in Louisiana than to take action. Also he quite failed to inform the admiral that after a visit to Baton Rouge he had reported his conclusions that his force was inadequate to take Port Hudson, and that the navy was not ready to cooperate.

This annoyed the old man no little; when Captain Thornton Jenkins reported aboard *Hartford* as the new flag captain on January 20, Farragut told him that the first object of the squadron must be to cut off the supplies of cattle, sheep, and corn from Texas to the Southern armies and a few strong ships above Port Hudson would do it. The period of inaction was abruptly ended by the news of the loss of *Queen of the West* and *Indianola;* Farragut made up his mind to get the heavy ships above Port Hudson, "army or no army." It was a typical Farragut out-of-hand operation. There had been losses in the Gulf and most of the vessels were in dreadful shape mechanically, but the new second-class screw sloop *Monongahela* joined, and the admiral moved up to Baton Rouge on March 11

with her, *Hartford, Richmond,* the old side-wheeler *Mississippi,* three 90-day gunboats, and six mortars.

On the afternoon of March 14 he was at anchor five
miles below Port Hudson, making arrangements, which
were for the three sloops to pass the forts in line, each with
a gunboat lashed to her port stern to furnish emergency
engine power, the side-wheeler to follow under her own
steam. The order was: *Hartford,* with *Albatross* (Lieutenant Commander John E. Hart), a merchant ship armed,
but so like a 90-day gunboat that there was no practical
difference; *Richmond* (Alden) with *Genesee* (Lieutenant
Commander P. C. Johnston); *Monongahela* (Captain J. P.
McKinstry) supported by *Kineo* (Lieutenant Commander
George M. Ransom); then *Mississippi* (Melancton Smith).
*Richmond* had the weakest engines of the big ships; *Genesee,* one of the curious double-enders, was the most powerful of the gunboats.

That afternoon there was an early dinner aboard and
all preparations were made; big boxes of sand placed next
to the guns to sop up any blood, brass rails and fittings
laid below, and all the interior decks whitewashed to give
whatever light there would be from reflection, since there
would be no other. The signal would be two red lights
under the stern of the flagship; they flashed at nine-thirty
and the ships began to move.

Port Hudson (which is not even on the map today) had
become very strong, with 8 24-pound English Whitworth
rifles, of comparatively small size but high penetration, 3
32-pounders, 2 42-pounders, 4 62-pounders, 2 8-inch, and
2 10-inch, 21 pieces in all, and plenty of time to fire them
as the ships came around the big bend of the Mississippi
from southwest, leaving a low point of land on their left,

while the eastern bluffs could dominate the stream by concentric fire. Farragut had some hope of slipping through in silence, close under the left bank, but this went glimmering when a Confederate outpost on the western shore sighted the ships and lighted a beacon. Well short of the dangerous right-angled turn, the batteries began to shoot; in reply *Hartford* opened a rolling fire, each gun in turn from bow to stern, so fast that the continuous glare picked out every detail of mast and spar. The ships behind accepted this as a signal for firing also; it was a muggy, misty night and they had no consciousness of where the batteries were until they could see the flash of the guns.

Now smoke began to gather over the stream, only *Hartford* in the lead free from it, the others taking increasing quantities of gun-cloud and funnel-cloud, with the location of the shore guns more dubious than ever. At the bend *Hartford* touched ground, bow to the eastern bank, but with *Albatross* backing while she went ahead, was pulled free and steamed on up, somewhat damaged in sides and spars, but with only one killed and two wounded. Less fortunate was *Richmond,* immediately behind; a shot went into her engine room, destroying her safety valve and releasing so much steam that there was neither pressure nor power, and *Genesee* could not hold her against the current. The two ships swung round and drifted downstream, while *Richmond's* gunners in that fog of war, not getting the word that they were turned in the opposite direction, fired at the flashes of *Mississippi's* guns instead of those from the bluffs.

*Monongahela* drew small-arms fire from the west bank as well as artillery from the heights. Her gunboat, *Kineo*, early lost its rudder; *Monongahela* could not carry the steering load for both against the fierce current and sheered into the bank. The shock was such that the ties to *Kineo* broke. Under heavy fire from the heights a hawser was rigged out and the gunboat pulled *Monongahela* loose; but no sooner had this been done than the sloop's crankpin overheated and the engines quit. Both ships drifted downstream together after *Richmond*, *Monongahela* with six killed and 21 wounded, much cut up.

Hardest of all was the beating *Mississippi* took. By the time she reached the critical area there was practically nothing at all to be seen; she fired and steamed and depended on the pilot. He had to use guesswork as to where to starboard his helm and the guess went wrong; *Mississippi* steamed into the west bank at full speed. There was no gunboat to help her and by this time bonfires were outlining the rigging of the big ship. For a full half-hour she tried to pull loose; then Melancton Smith gave orders for the crew to be taken off in boats and the frigate to be fired. The exec was Lieutenant George Dewey, himself to be an admiral and a hero one day; he managed to persuade some reluctant rowers to return to the burning ship and get out the last live men, including a frightened ship's boy who had hid under a pile of dead.

The burning *Mississippi* later worked herself free and drifted exploding down the stream, which was doubtless the reason Farragut sent Melancton Smith away out of his command. He was a singular character, completely encompassed in his own concept of what regulations demanded of him. It was noted that at the passage of the New Orleans forts he steamed around the river until he could get Farragut's permission to attack *Manassas,* then promptly destroyed her.

The total result of the operation can be viewed as a

microcosm of the Civil War. The Confederates had gained a showy tactical victory, which would give them a good talking point; of seven ships that started to pass Port Hudson, one was destroyed and four driven back disabled. But the two that got through with Farragut altered the strategic position by setting up a blockade of the Red River; no supplies moved down to Vicksburg or Port Hudson thereafter and shortages began to appear, not to mention the armies farther east. "Great God! How unfortunate!" was the word from one of General Dick Taylor's commissaries up the Red. "Four steamers arrived today from Shreveport. One had a load of 300,000 pounds of bacon, three others are reported coming down with loads. Five others are below with full cargoes designed for Port Hudson, but it is reported that the Federal gunboats are blockading the river."

*Webb* and *Queen of the West* were still upstream; Farragut made his usually ingeniously careful preparations to avoid what had happened to *Indianola.* He lowered all the lower yards to the deck, lashed them there, and carried a heavy chain from the bowsprit right around from yard-tip to yard-tip, to keep an attacker 15 or 20 feet from the ship; heavy cypress logs were slung against the sides, a foot from the waterline; and, as close-in protection, hawsers were slung from the lower rigging, 30 feet above the deck, and heavy boarding netting carried down to the rail. There were some odd-looking ships in the Mississippi squadron, but *Hartford,* dressed out like this, must have been one of the oddest.

Still the old man was not satisfied. He wanted a couple of fast rams to make the Red River blockade tight, and communicated with Grant, who said he would make things right with Porter, so *Lancaster* (John A. Ellet) and

*Switzerland* (C. R. Ellet) were selected to run the batteries. For some reason known only to the officers of the Marine Brigade, they decided to start at seven in the morning. The result was that it was full daylight when they were opposite Vicksburg. *Lancaster,* an old boat and fragile, was hit in the boilers, run into the bank, and destroyed; *Switzerland* got through damaged and was of much use in the river blockade.

However, nothing could "make things right with Porter" when he found out that the run had been made in daylight, and simultaneously there arrived a letter from A. W. Ellet, saying that the Marine Brigade would prefer to serve under army command. This was just one too many pieces of Marine Brigade impudence. The admiral had A. W. Ellet arrested at once and, only after the brigadier general had withdrawn his letter, relented enough to send the whole command up the Tennessee to chase guerrillas.

Banks, meanwhile, had moved up to Alexandria, Louisiana, decided there was nothing doing there, and came back to blockade Port Hudson on the land side. It was not a very active siege, but the place was now down to what supplies were already inside.

## II

As far back as February, Grant had contemplated cutting through the west bank into an old course of the Mississippi named Lake Providence, deepening and widening it down to where it communicated with the Red, then landing on the east bank from the river, with the new channel as his line of communications. It was soon evident that this was not going to jell; the Lake Providence cutoff ran out into widespread morass that did not afford floating water for ships. Grant merely kept the men at work on it

for occupation during the period when Porter's gunboats
tried the Yazoo Pass and Steele's Bayou routes.

The failure of these efforts made it clear that a new
basic solution was needed. Grant asked Porter whether he
could shoot enough gunboats through Vicksburg to guar-
antee a landing on the east bank if the army marched
down the Louisiana shore for a crossing. Being told that
Navy would take care of that part, he called a council of
war and proposed his new plan: to land on the high
ground below Vicksburg, abandon communications if necessary, and fight his way into the rear of the fortress. Every
divisional commander was against it and Sherman presented a very able paper showing how impossible such a
move would be. Grant listened to all, then said: "I am
sorry to differ with you all, but my mind is made up; the
army will move tomorrow at ten o'clock."

McClernand's corps led down the right bank through
enormous difficulties, building bridges at every step, and
early in April was at New Carthage. Porter began by loading cotton around the boilers of his gunboats, topping it
with bags of hay and grain, which besides being a protection would come in handy to the troops below. Three
transports would be taken to see if they could stand the
racket, and at ten o'clock on the night of April 15 the
expedition started. *Benton* (Lieutenant Commander James
A. Greer) led with Porter aboard; then the new, fine
*Lafayette* (Walke), with *General Price* (Lieutenant Commander Selim Woodworth) lashed to her off side, *Louisville* (Lieutenant Commander E. K. Owen), *Mound City*
(Byron Wilson), *Pittsburg* (Hoel), *Carondelet* (Murphy),
followed by the transports, with the new *Tuscumbia*
(Shirk) bringing up the rear to cover emergencies.

Porter's plan was to drift close under the batteries and

get as far as possible without being seen. This succeeded well at the upper works, but as the ships moved lower down, tar barrels began to blaze at the foot of the Vicksburg bluffs, the railroad station on the opposite shore was fired, and everything became light and a pandemonium of guns. The transport *Henry Clay* was disabled in her engines, her cotton-bale armor was set afire, and she burned up; but grape from the ships made the batteries inaccurate, all the rest were at New Carthage by two-thirty in the morning, counting hits and finding a total of 68, but no serious damage. The fleets were met for the second time, but Admiral Porter was spared meeting his detested brother; "Dirty Bill" had gone home with an illness from which he would never recover, though it took him nearly a year to die of it.

McClernand was supposed to push on at once and be covered by Porter's ships while he crossed to take Grand Gulf, but he moved forward only as far as a place called Perkins' Plantation and went into camp. Porter got aboard *General Price* and went down to reconnoiter Grand Gulf. He drew only two shots from a fieldpiece but saw many big guns lying ashore, waiting to be mounted, and advised McClernand to cross at once. The politician-general talked learnedly of lines of communication and turned down the advice.

Grant arrived five days later, with part of the second corps, McPherson's, coming along behind. By this time five additional transports had run the batteries, though with damage that reduced some of them to barges which had to be towed. The command was forward; the troops to be placed aboard transports to be landed as soon as the gunboats had silenced the Grand Gulf artillery. But this was no longer very easy to do. The Confederates had now mounted 1 100-pounder, 2 64-pounders, 2 7-inch rifles, 3 30-pound Parrott rifles, 2 20-pounders and 1 10-pound Parrott rifle. On the morning of April 29 *Pittsburg, Mound City, Louisville,* and *Carondelet* attacked the lower batteries, while *Benton, Tuscumbia,* and *Lafayette* went in against the upper.

It was early found that the gunboats had taken on an assignment too heavy for them. The upper gunboats, fighting downstream, sheered back and forth with the current and could get no accurate aim; the lower ones could not reach the heights. After five hours the Confederate guns remained unsilenced, and all the ships had damage. *Tuscumbia* was hit 81 times, the shells came through her ports and the sides where the miserably attached armor fell off to kill six, wound 24, and disable her engines; *Benton* was hit 47 times, losing nine killed and two wounded; the stout *Lafayette* had 47 hits but only one wounded; *Pittsburg* 35 hits, with six killed and 13 wounded.

It was clear that Grand Gulf was a failure, as Fort Donelson had been, and would not be taken this day or this way. Grant decided to go farther downstream still; early on the morning of April 30 McClernand's corps and one division of McPherson landed on the east bank at Bruinsburg with four days' rations and began to march.

At the same time other transports carried Sherman's corps into the Yazoo for what was to look like another try at Haines' Bluff, and Lieutenant Commander Breese in *Black Hawk* led a squadron of gunboats in support—*De Kalb* (Walker), the new *Choctaw* (Lieutenant Commander F. M. Ramsay), *Tyler* (Prichett), with the tinclads *Signal* (Dominy), *Romeo* (Lieutenant J. V. Johnston), *Linden* (Lieutenant T. E. Smith), and *Petrel* (Lieutenant John Pierce), and three mortars. The gunboats made a lively and noisy show; *Tyler* got a shot below the water line and had to pull out for repairs, but *Choctaw* proved as stout as her sister *Lafayette,* taking 47 hits without damage, and ironclads and mortars hammered so heavily that the Confederates almost ceased fire, while some of the troops debarked. The objective was fully achieved; General Pemberton, commanding the fortress, got reports indicating that Haines' Bluff was the main point of attack, and scattered his forces so much that he never did get them together again until after Grant began to hit him. Then it was too late.

### III

On May 3 Porter dropped down to the mouth of the Red for a conference with Farragut. With so many ironclads between the two fortresses, there was no reason why the ocean admiral should stay; he left *Hartford* under Porter's command rather than run her through Port Hudson again, and went southward overland to join his deep ships and be out of this story. Porter took *Benton, Lafayette,* and *Pittsburg* up the Red, where the Confederates had a fort covering the line to Alexandria, Fort De Russy, with iron-plated casemates like those at Arkansas Post. Experience at the latter place had deprived the rebels of any confidence in what such a work could accomplish against armored ships; they dismounted their guns and went away. Two ironclads were left in the river to make its blockade complete.

On Porter's return he found Grant had taken Grand Gulf from the rear; the admiral switched over to the upper squadron with his flag in *Black Hawk* and began poking up the Yazoo. On May 15 there was the sound of firing in the distance; shortly after, soldiers could be seen jumping up and down on the unattainable bluffs and they wore the Union blue—Sherman's corps, driving the rebels into the city and cutting off the batteries at Haines' Bluff, which presently fell with all their guns and stores. As soon as the gullet could be cleared of torpedoes, which was by the 20th, Porter sent Walke up to see how things were coming at Yazoo City, with *De Kalb* and the tinclads *New National* (Master Alexander M. Grant), *Kenwood* (Master John Swaney), and *Signal*, taking a force of troops.

They found the place a smoking desolation, Isaac Brown having no real defense, so that he was compelled to burn his three rams on the stocks. He was a most unlucky man; able, intelligent, courageous, with a good gift of command, but all his enterprises came to nothing. *De Kalb* and the tinclads ranged up the river and its tributaries, destroying steamers and taking stores. Navigation on the Yazoo ceased.

On May 21 Grant came out to confer with Porter; he was going to assault Vicksburg the next morning and wanted an hour's supporting fire from the gunboats. Porter thought mortars would be more effective, but went in against the hill batteries with *Benton, Tuscumbia, Mound City,* and *Carondelet,* and did pretty well, silencing a number of pieces and actually knocking out two or three big guns, stopping only because he began to run out of ammunition. *Mound City* took hits that broke two of her guns, *Benton* was hit 13 times without being penetrated, and of course the worthless *Tuscumbia* was disabled again and driven out of action.

Grant's assault was a failure; he settled down to a siege, with the gunboats and mortars supporting from the river at long range. There is little history for this stage; it was simply hard dog-work, each ship in turn by day or night going in to throw shells into the city and drawing little return. But on 29 May Sherman asked for help against a water battery that was preventing him from extending his right flank. His belief was that the heavy guns on the heights above had been taken away to cover the land face, where he had been pressing the Confederates hard. Porter sent in *Cincinnati,* under his nephew, G. M. Bache. The moment she got into range it was revealed that the upper guns had merely been lowered behind the parapets and about half a dozen 8- and 10-inch opened up on her. The first shot went right through the upper deck and out the ship's bottom; she began to sink at once, while more and more of the heavy shot tore into her. Bache swung his ship around and began to crawl out of action at three knots, but before she got very far she went down, taking 15 of the crew with her in addition to 20 others killed by enemy fire. Her guns were raised later and mounted in a battery manned by sailors in the rear of Vicksburg.

The sinking of *Cincinnati* was the last gasp of the fortress. On July 4 Grant marched into Vicksburg, with bands playing and national salutes being fired from ships and shore, then came out for dinner aboard *Black Hawk.* Port Hudson surrendered four days later; there were serenades on the White House lawn; and Lincoln proclaimed: "The Father of Waters once more flows unvexed to the sea." To Grant the credit and the glory; but it may be noted that the gunboats gave him a mobility his opponents did not have. They never got any help from the trans-Mississippi command, although it was ordered.

# 10

# Small War

AFTER THE FALL of Vicksburg the war on the rivers takes
on an entirely different character. The Confederates no
longer had anything afloat except the hidden-away *Webb*
and no further forts or posts except up the Red and its
adjunct streams. That is, Jefferson Davis' defense system
in the west had collapsed; at any point within reach of
water deep enough for a gunboat, Union troops could be
delivered with all needed logistic support. Powerful Confederate armies still existed in the interior, but they approached the invisible seacoast of the Mississippi system
at their peril, and they stood no chance of crossing the
big river in force—or, for that matter, any of its major
branches. The movable fortress of the navy placed heavy
artillery everywhere.

But the existence of those Confederate armies, the facts
that they were provided with strong wings of cavalry and

were generally supported by the population, permitted
and indicated attack on Union river communications by
guerrilla bands supported by regular troops. Against this,
again the defense was naval, the more necessary because
the passage of reinforcements and logistic support were
primarily waterborne. Paved roads there were none; and
at least down to November of 1863 what railroads there
were suffered from lack of connections and a wild variety
of gauges.

There resulted a long series of actions in which men
died as bravely or miserably as in the trenches of Vicksburg or on the decks of *Cincinnati,* but without ponder-
able individual effect except on the casualty lists. On the
Tennessee and Cumberland, indeed, the new phase began
as early as January, 1863, just after the Battle of Stone
River, when the impact of that exhausting struggle suddenly burdened the lines of support for Rosecrans' Army
of the Cumberland at Nashville. Porter was downstream
with Grant at the time and communications to him were
intolerably slow; the general short-circuited by writing to
Captain Alexander Pennock at the Cairo-Mound City base,
asking for more gunboat convoy for his troop and supply
shipments.

The immediate occasion for the demand was a fairly
disgraceful incident in January, less than two weeks after
Stone River, when Wheeler's cavalry of Bragg's command
stopped the hospital ship *Trio* at Harpeth Shoals and then
halted a couple of supply ships following behind her. "A
gang of drunken rebels came on board and proceeded to
rob the boat and wounded of everything movable. I demanded of Colonel Wade, their commander, an explanation, but he, being drunk, only gave an idiotic reply." The
tinclad *W. H. Sidell* (Lieutenant William Van Dorn) pres-

ently appeared; whether from consideration for the
wounded or for his own hide, he failed to fire a shot, and
the river being blocked by the other ship, his vessel was
captured and burned with the rest, while he himself was
taken prisoner and disappears from all record.

This Pennock of Mound City was a man now 50, who
had fought the pirates of Quallah Battoo and done much
time in the lighthouse-inspection service, where he gained
a reputation for administrative capacity. Foote recommended him to Davis; Davis similarly praised him when
he transferred the command to Porter; and Porter, who
found fault with so many men and things, never found
any with Pennock, and gave him the general direction of
affairs on Ohio, Tennessee, and Cumberland, subject only
to policy revisions.

Pennock already had Lieutenant Commander Leroy
Fitch patrolling the rivers with three tinclads when the
*Trio* incident occurred and now added two more, giving
the command *Fairplay, Brilliant, St. Clair, Silver Lake,*
and *Robb.* He also sent on Phelps with *Lexington,* that
ship having been brought north for repairs, somewhat
wracked after the attack on Arkansas Post. Phelps was
supposed to go in only for a survey, but of course when
he got into Rosecrans' area there was always another job
for him and he was never released.

He left Cairo early in 1863 and went up to Nashville.
Twenty miles above Clarksville, where he landed a party
to burn a storehouse, he was hit three times by a mobile
Parrott gun without serious damage. There were, naturally, some Union men in divided Tennessee and Phelps
was a good interrogator; he was able to report with some
certainty: "The rebels have a number of guns, with considerable covering force, extending along Harpeth Shoals

a distance of eight or ten miles. This force can readily operate on both the Cumberland and Tennessee." His recommendation was that no transport should pass Henry or Donelson without gunboat convoy and that *Lexington* be left in the eastern rivers, because the Confederate shore artillery usually did not mind firing on transports under cover of the tinclads, but disappeared rapidly when the big guns came into play.

Pennock now organized a system of large convoys, covered by *Lexington* and the five tinclads. One of these was moving up the Cumberland late on February 6, when a steamer came down in a hurry, saying that Colonel A. C. Harding with 800 men at Fort Donelson was under heavy attack and had used up all his artillery ammunition. Fitch dropped the convoy and speeded up his warships; they arrived at eight in the evening to find the rebels massed in a ravine and graveyard from north around to west of the place, ready for an assault—Wheeler's cavalry of Bragg's army, 4500 strong, now mostly dismounted. The situation was made to order for the gunboats, which opened an enfilading fire along the ravine and into the graveyard, while *Lexington* used her heavy pieces to throw shells over the graveyard into a hollow behind, where the rebels had their horses. The fire of more than 30 pieces of artillery, delivered at complete surprise was more than any troops could stand; the Confederates decamped, leaving 100 prisoners and 140 dead behind. Wheeler wrote a report in which he placed the blame on the fact that some of his men thought the Yankees were trying to steal their horses; "abandoned their favorable position and rushed back to protect them." It barely mentioned the gunboats.

Harding got a brigadier's commission; Fitch got only an opportunity for more work. His report on February 9

lists 73 steamers and 16 barges convoyed to Nashville, but
even this was not enough for Rosecrans, who wanted more
gunboats, more supplies, more convoys. The general went
beyond channels to wire Lincoln direct that Van Dorn's
cavalry was menacing his communications (Van Dorn was
actually in Mississippi, facing Grant), and it was "absolutely necessary" that the gunboats be under his local commanders. This was a violation of the chain of command
and a clear case of empire-building, but it brought forth
a snowstorm of telegrams in all directions, the end product
of which were a report from Fitch, detailing his arrangements (he was taking all his ships out of the Ohio and
making up convoys weekly), and news from Pennock that
the new tinclad *Springfield* had been assigned.

The base captain was purchasing and fitting out new
ships as fast as ever he could and by the end of the year
had added 26, including several little stern-wheelers that
drew only 16 inches, for operations up the smaller rivers.
But not every ship was suitable, and there was constant
trouble with the constructors; as late as May '63 Phelps
was reporting to Porter from a new tinclad that: "Mr.
Joseph Brown's work is of the most worthless description"
and Master Carpenter Kendall of Cincinnati was not fit
for his position. (Brown seems to have had pull of some
mysterious kind; none of the naval officers liked the work
he did, but he kept right on getting contracts.)

Yet the presence of the tinclads exerted a restraining
effect; the only action recorded in those early months of
1863 after the Donelson episode came on April 2, when
some rebel artillery at Palmyra opened on a small convoy
in charge of *Fairplay* and *St. Clair*. *St. Clair* lost a steampipe and one man; the other gunboat met her drifting
down, and went back to shell out and burn the place

which could not have made a very good blaze as its population was 133. No more than one or two men of the elusive mobile forces were caught. The report reached Porter at about the time he began to have trouble with Alfred Ellet of the Marine Brigade, and simultaneously there was a letter from Grant, suggesting that the Brigade operate up the Tennessee. Ellet's orders sent him in in mid-April, with his troops and the rams *Monarch, Lioness, Horner,* and *Dick Fulton,* the ships now having light howitzers on their upper decks. It was to be a counter-offensive operation.

*Covington, Queen City,* and *Argosy,* the new 16-inch gunboats, were ready; with them Fitch convoyed the Marine Brigade up the Tennessee all the way to Florence-Tuscumbia, where they were joined by a land force sent by General Grenville Dodge of the Corinth command; and the local rebel concentration was broken up after a sharp little fight. The water was falling; Ellet and his rams dropped back downstream again, pausing to destroy flat-boats and ferries wherever they could be found. On April 16 in the morning, being off Duck River Shoals, the rams were suddenly set upon by artillery and musketry from the shore, the Confederates having evidently mistaken them for transports. The Confederates were quickly un-deceived; the Marine Brigade poured ashore under cover of its shipboard howitzers and drove the rebels from the field under cavalry pursuit. But the water had now become so low that the rams could no longer operate; the Marine Brigade steamed back down the Mississippi and on 29 May joined Grant in the siege of Vicksburg.

On May 4 command of the minor rivers was divided, Ledyard Phelps taking the Tennessee with *Covington, Queen City, Argosy, Silver Cloud,* and *Champion,* while

Fitch had the Ohio and Cumberland with the other ships. There was little fighting on either river except for some shooting at Cerro Gordo on June 19, when Phelps heard there were some guerrillas in the neighborhood, and landed several guns with a force to support them. The rebels, apparently taking this for a foraging party and not knowing of the guns, attacked as soon as the gunboats were out of sight around a bend; they were well pounded.

Later in the month Master S. F. Handford of *Little Rebel* (now a part of the command) learned that a party of Confederate cavalry with guns would lie in wait for tinclads, proposing to give them one round from each piece, and then make off. Handford landed two howitzers from his ship at the spot where the Confederates were supposed to appear, then steamed upstream, where *Silver Lake* and *Robb* were on patrol. When the sound of the guns was heard the tinclads turned back down and opened fire against the rebels just coming in, four abreast. They left 50 dead.

This was typical of the period; the fact was that after the Marine Brigade broke up the supporting combination, the Confederates had difficulty maintaining their light forces. Guerrilla activity did not altogether cease, and the gunboats anchored in mid-stream at night, but there was less willingness to take a chance on running into something that might have artillery.

A change of pace came in July with John Morgan's famous cavalry raid into Indiana and Ohio. At this time Fitch had sent *Lexington* to the lower Ohio in the Paducah region. Being warned that Morgan was on the loose, he had *Fairplay* and *Silver Lake* patrolling the river between Evansville and Shawneetown, *Springfield* between Evansville and Louisville, and *St. Clair* and *Brilliant* between

Smithland and Shawneetown. Three new small ships, *Moose, Reindeer,* and *Victory,* had just taken their crews aboard at Cincinnati when Fitch learned that the raider had crossed the Ohio and was in Indiana with 6000 cavalry. The naval officer summoned *Fairplay* and *Silver Lake* upstream by telegraph and himself started down for the danger spot with *Moose* and *Victory.*

*Springfield* (Ensign Joseph Watson) made the first contact near Brandenburg on the 9th, where she was fired on by infantry and a battery of guns on a high hill; her return fire was ineffective. It was obvious to Fitch that Morgan would stay on the move, and he guessed that the move would be upstream, which turned out to be perfectly accurate, the Confederate leader having decided that he had better reach a point where gunboats could not follow him across the bars of summer low water.

They should not in fact have been able to, but Fitch and some of his men worked out one of the maddest naval inventions ever conceived on the spot. Two spars were carried forward and down from the bow of a gunboat and then hove taut; steam being applied, the ship rode onward and up over the bar as on a pair of crutches. It was called "jumping"; with it Fitch and his tinclads followed the raiders upstream, keeping abreast of their right flank with *Moose,* presently joined by *Reindeer* and the new *Naumkeag. Springfield* and *Victory* kept ahead of the moving troops and *Fairplay* and *Silver Lake* followed behind. "This might have been considered an extravagant use of boats, but the river was so low and the fords so numerous that a less number might not have met with such a favorable result."

On the night of the 18th *Moose* was at Sand Creek Bar, below Buffington Island, while the others were guarding

various shoal fords up and down. At two in the morning
Fitch jumped his ship across the bar and moved upstream;
at seven a dense fog lifted to show part of Morgan's men
coming downstream fast with some artillery. Fitch shelled
them and they removed; a little later and farther up he
found a column nearly a third of the way across, drove it
back with many casualties, and took two pieces of artillery
on the bank. Next morning General Scammon's Union infantry came up in transports; Fitch steamed on, caught a
group of Confederates trying to cross, and broke them up.
Morgan's command was tattering out; 14 miles farther up
two small squads of not over 40 did get across the river,
pursued by shellfire from *Moose,* but most of the remainder did not, and thanks to the naval blockade Morgan
and the balance of his men were taken in small packages
by the assembling pursuit.

During the wars of the French Revolution cavalry captured Dutch ships (they were locked in ice); this is probably the only occasion when naval vessels reversed the
process.

## II

The war on the Mississippi and its more southern tributaries assumed the same character as that in Kentucky-
Tennessee; an affair of ambushes and sudden attacks,
retaliation from the tinclads and gunboats, burnt-out plantation houses and fallow fields where sugar and cotton had
once been tall. The ships took care of that problem in
detail; the one that drove Porter to distraction was how to
deal with the insect-swarm of speculators who followed the
steamer *Imperial* when she, first of all, completed the trip
from St. Louis to New Orleans on July 16. Lincoln was
trying to reconstruct in the Mississippi basin area while

he carried on the war in others; the orders were to treat people well, try to rent the vacant plantations, and allow reasonable trade, mainly in provisions and household goods. Treasury agents were in charge; they supplied clearances at Memphis and St. Louis.

At this point, enter greed. What the traders wanted was cotton, higher in price than ever in history, and by God they were going to have it. They possessed a powerful lobby in Washington, which succeeded in persuading Treasury to issue a circular of regulations so complicated that it would have taken the Supreme Court years to interpret it. Actual interpretation was in the hands of an augmented cloud of Treasury agents, who needed money and could get it from cotton speculators. The total result was that anyone who wanted to trade, traded—"a greater pack of villains never went unhung," Porter wrote to Sherman. Fortunes were made, and even the guerrillas who needed ammunition came down to the river bank by appointment to give cotton for it. Sometimes after a cheery drink aboard, they took what they wanted and burned the boats, reports of which never made Porter unhappy. As a matter of fact, most of the river guerrillas, theoretically Confederate patriots, were out for their own hands, though there were all sorts of borderline cases. In actions important enough to merit official report there were usually involved formations with names, numbers, and musterrolls; the real guerrillas were small-time operators.

During this period Selfridge and his *Conestoga* succeeded in altering geography and history. At the mouth of the Arkansas was a long, narrow point projecting into the Mississippi, making an 18-mile turn necessary to get around it, a favorite haunt of rifle-armed guerrillas, who enjoyed firing at transports in the stream out of pure de-

structive malice. One morning Selfridge noticed that the
high water had partly flooded the neck across this point;
it occurred to him that very little more would be needed
to give the river a new course. He landed a boat's crew;
they dug a couple hundred yards of ditch and next
morning the Mississippi was cutting through, already so
deep and swift that it carried *Conestoga* down at 12 knots,
barely able to steer. The transports he left at the entrance
to the cutoff were dumfounded to find *Conestoga* around
the bend before them. The alteration ultimately carried
away the whole town of Napoleon, one of the most famous
gambling headquarters of old steamboat days, and the
owners of the gambling hells threatened to sue Selfridge
for damages after the war. They had trouble finding a
lawyer to take their case.

On May 23, while A. W. Ellet was coming down the
Mississippi with his Marine Brigade, his quartermaster
boat was fired on by two pieces of artillery near Austin,
Mississippi. He landed 200 marine cavalry and scouted
the country till he came on a body of Confederate horse;
there was a fight in which each side reported repulsing the
other, after losing about 20 men. While it was going on,
Ellet burned Austin; concealed weapons in some of the
houses went off like a drumfire of musketry.

Also during the Vicksburg campaign were the doings
at Simmesport, Louisiana. General Banks heard something
was going on there and asked for naval reconnaissance
into the Atchalfaya. Walke, who was in local command,
sent the ram *Switzerland* (John A. Ellet) on the morning
of June 3; she found some breastworks behind the levee,
was received with a fire her howitzers could not master,
and pulled out with her steam-escape pipe cut, cotton
armor afire, and three wounded. When Walke got Ellet's

report he asked for troops to mop up the situation, and, not getting them, took *Pittsburg* in himself. Now the overmatch was reversed; after a little firing from the great guns the rebels ran away and Walke landed demolition parties to burn their camp and buildings.

The affair at Milliken's Bend was a serious attack. Grant had made the place a forward base for stores, defended by the 5th, 49th and 51st regiments of the new colored troops and the 23rd Iowa. On June 6 word reached Porter that the rebels were milling around in the background in a highly menacing manner. He sent *Choctaw* (Lieutenant Commander F. M. Ramsay) and as an afterthought dispatched Bache with *Lexington* behind her. Ramsay and his ship arrived to find the levee so high they could not see over it, but got around that one by mooring his vessel in the stream and stationing a couple of men on the bank to give hand signals.

At three-fifteen in the morning an officer hailed to say that the pickets were driven in, and then came the sound of firing, though not very much of it, because the Negro troops on the line of resistance broke at the first onset and ran away to hide under the bank, pursued by two brigades of yelling rebels who took no prisoners. *Choctaw* opened with 100-pound percussion shell and five-second fuses from the 9-inch, firing slowly. The Confederates did not like that very well; they tried various devices of flanking and encirclement, but when they opened out they could do nothing with the Iowa regiment, and when they tried to mass the big guns took them. By eight-thirty it was all over, and when *Lexington* arrived soon after, it was only in time to encourage the rebel retreat. They left 98 dead behind.

The troops who made this attack, two brigades under

General J. G. Walker, described as "a half-naked, half-starving set," wandered north-northwest from their defeat, and on June 29 made a try at another of Grant's depots, at Goodrich's Landing, about ten miles below Lake Providence. Here too, the defenders were colored troops; but the rebels were now more interested in plunder than in victory and were quite thoroughly occupied with rifling and burning plantations when there arrived *John Raine* (Major Hubbard of the Marine Brigade). The Confederates took her for a transport and opened fire from light howitzers, were no little discomfited at receiving reply from 12-pounder brass rifles, and still more so when the tinclad *Romeo* (Lieutenant J. V. Johnston) appeared. A retreat began, apparently not carried through with speed or order, since when General A. W. Ellet came with the whole Marine Brigade at two in the morning, the Confederates were still in the neighborhood. Ellet landed the brigade and followed as far as the Tensas, where the Confederates had burned the bridge and thrown up forts on the opposite side. As Ellet's was an essentially naval force, he went back to the stream.

These operations, though carried out by regular troops, were essentially smash-and-grab guerrilla raids. The attack on Helena, cooked up by General T. H. Holmes of the Confederate trans-Mississippi command, was a regular operation, designed as a diversionary move to help Vicksburg and, if all went well, to recover a line of communications across the river. Porter, who had developed a remarkably good technique of personally questioning deserters and contrabands, heard of it from one of them on June 21, and at once ordered to the spot *Tyler* (Prichett), *General Bragg* (Lieutenant Joshua Bishop) and *Hastings* (Lieutenant A. R. Langthorne). General B. M. Prentiss, in charge of the post, was no little surprised to hear he would shortly be attacked by over three times his numbers, but expressed confidence in his ability to hold out without help. *Bragg* anchored off the town; *Tyler* and *Hastings* began to cruise up and down in quest of guerrillas.

After several days of this Bishop of *Bragg* got bored and asked Prentiss permission to go up to Memphis and repair his engines, which were in bad shape. Prentiss said he still didn't think there would be any attack, and told him to go ahead. At about the same time Prichett reread his orders, discovered they were peremptory as to staying at Helena, and returned to take a position where he could best cover the town. This was just as well; he had hardly anchored on the morning of July 4 when the rebels came on in overwhelming force, carried a commanding hill, and began to mass for a general assault from three directions, along the ravines in the center and from batteries in the wings.

Prichett cleverly placed *Tyler* where her bow guns bore on one set of batteries, her stern guns on the other, with the big broadside 8-inch on the ravine of the Confederate concentration. The heavy shells tore Holmes' troops to pieces; by twelve-thirty he was going back and Prentiss was counterattacking. He took 900 prisoners; 600 dead were found in the ravine where *Tyler's* shells had fallen so heavily; and Prentiss was so much impressed that he wrote to ask for Prichett's promotion.

Holmes' forces began moving north, drawing supplies through Little Rock. Word of this reached Washington; Halleck wired Prentiss to draw in reinforcements from Grant and cut off the rebel force, asking for gunboat help up the White, while General Schofield of the Missouri command closed in from that state. Porter sent *Marmora, Cricket, Linden,* and *Romeo,* the whole headed by Bache in *Lexington,* to which he had been appointed after *Cincinnati* went down. The ships moved in in the later days of July. There was no fighting, the Union forces ashore and afloat being entirely too heavy, though there was the usual sporadic sniping and one man in the fleet was wounded. At the mouth of the Little Red, a narrow and tortuous branch of the White, Bache heard of two fine steamers up the stream. He sent *Cricket* (A. R. Langthorne), the smallest of the tinclads, and she returned with her prizes on August 16; they were the only means the Confederates had of moving more than a handful of men on the river.

When Grant closed in Vicksburg, General Joe Johnston made fairly vigorous efforts to effect a relief, and one of the steps he took was to reoccupy Yazoo City, setting up a battery of a single 6-inch gun and some small pieces. Isaac Brown was still on hand. Before Walke's expedition up the stream in May, the people of Yazoo City told him that if he planted any of his infernal machines in "their" river they would hang him. But the Federal attacks changed their minds; they allowed him to install some of his "fretwells" at the point where a ship would have to lie to fire on the battery, while repair work was begun on ships hiding up the branches. On July 13, Vicksburg safely in Union hands, Lieutenant Commander Walker was sent up the Yazoo to see about that battery with his own *Baron De Kalb, New National* (Master Alexander M. Grant), *Kenwood* (Master John Swaney), and *Signal* (Dominy), with 5000 troops. As *De Kalb* moved into position but before she could do any firing, a torpedo went off under her bow and almost immediately another under her stern. There was no chance of saving her; Walker got her into the bank and began taking out what could be preserved of guns and stores. Not a man was lost and neither was there any firing; the rebels moved on at the sight of the Union troops; and all the ships in the Yazoo tributaries were burned. The chief result of the affair was that ten days later Porter issued a general order in which he prescribed that each ship should protect herself against torpedoes with a huge rake borne on a 20-foot spar under the bows. It didn't work.

An extensive system of streams—the Tensas, Bayou Macon, Black River—flows through the lowlands west of Vicksburg, winding south almost parallel with the greater stream till they fall into the Washita. When Confederate General Walker's command was driven from Goodrich's Landing, they established themselves in this area and around Tensas Lake and did what they could by firing on Mississippi shipping. They were safe against counter-attack until after the fall of Vicksburg, when Porter dispatched an expedition under Selfridge, with his flag in *Conestoga* and the tinclads *Rattler* (Master W. E. H. Fentress), *Forest Rose* (Master George W. Brown), *Petrel* (Master Charles S. Kenrick), *Marmora* (Lieutenant Robert Getty), *Curlew* (Ensign A. B. O'Neill), and *Manitou* (ex-*Fort Hindman* (Lieutenant John Pearce). Selfridge pushed up the Tensas on July 12 with his tinclads and surprised his opponents. Some small Confederate transports were ahead, but they mostly escaped into intricate uncharted channels. A big depot of stores was taken, there was a little shooting, and next morning Selfridge divided, sending *Manitou* and *Rattler* up the Little Red, which falls into the Black, while *Forest Rose* and *Petrel* climbed the Tensas toward the lake.

*Manitou* and her teammate found the steamer *Louisville,* last big river ship remaining to the Confederacy, and brought her back to be converted into a tinclad with the odd armament of 40 small brass howitzers. *Forest Rose* and *Petrel* captured a steamer with a cargo of sugar and rum. On the 14th Selfridge ran up the Washita with *Conestoga* and *Manitou* (which, unlike the other tinclads carried 8-inch guns) and threw a few shells into a fort at Harrisonburg, but it was too heavily armed for wooden gunboats, so they came back.

By October, *Osage* was ready, first of the new river monitors. She came down to the mouth of the Red under Lieutenant J. P. Couthouy, where on the 7th a deserter brought in information that the Confederates had a steamer coming down. Couthouy sent 20 of his men armed with rifles cross-country under the guidance of a contraband. They found the steamer *Argus* on the opposite side of the stream; she surrendered after three shots, and they were just putting out a boat party to seize her when another ship was heard coming. Chief Engineer Thomas Doughty, who was in charge of the party, hid his men behind some bushes until she came down, a fine big sidewheeler named *Robert Fulton*, only completed at the beginning of the war. Confederate General Dick Taylor was trying to smuggle her through to be used in transporting troops across the Atchalfaya. She too surrendered to the rifle-armed seamen; as the water was slack and rebel forces would assemble before the ships could be worked across the bar at the mouth of the Red, both were burned.

In September there took place the violent Battle of Chickamauga and Rosecrans' Army of the Cumberland was driven back and besieged in Chattanooga. This brought a good deal of river-naval movement. Welles asked Porter to send gunboats to cover the transport of supplies and troops across the Tennessee at Florence;

Sherman and his corps were hurrying from the west to Chattanooga. Porter replied that the river was at its slackest, there were only 22 inches of water over the shoals, but he would do what he could. On October 21 Phelps reached Eastport with *Hastings* and *Key West,* covering the transports for the crossing and bringing in supplies.

Sherman appreciated it too. "I am never easy with a railroad," he wrote, "which takes a whole army to guard, every foot of rail being essential to the whole; whereas they can't stop the Tennessee, and each boat can make its own game." Now the rivers began to rise and down to the fighting around Chattanooga the operations were supported by *Lexington* and five of the tinclads—*Key West, Cricket, Robb, Hastings, Peosta.* The importance of their presence lay not in what happened but in what failed to happen; the thundercloud from which Grant discharged his terrible lightning against Missionary Ridge was assembled without let or hindrance, the supplies passed through, the river crossings were held secure.

In November the Confederates became active around the mouth of the Red, where the bar prohibited entry without special preparation. Dominy of *Signal* took a 9-inch on a flatboat in tow and went up to the mouth on November 17. He was fired on 18 times, had five men wounded, and his ship was somewhat beaten up; but he gave better than he took. When *Choctaw* presently came up to join him, the rebel batteries were driven to cover with casualties.

The next day the transport *Emerald* was fired on in the same general region; *Kenwood* and *Lafayette* relieved her and drove the Confederate artillery away. It came back on the 21st to fire on the transport *Black Hawk* (not Porter's flagship but an army vessel) and drove her aground with tiller ropes cut, but *Choctaw* again appeared and forced the rebels to conclude that this form of attack was not a paying proposition.

. . . What do these piddling actions, these few men killed, these few shells fired, add up to? This: one of the great historical dangers in the Civil War was that even if the Union won, it might settle down into an embittered conflict of guerrillas and repression, growing into intolerable savagery on both sides, as with Napoleon in Spain. God knows, there was enough guerrilla raiding on one side and barn-burning on the other in our internecine conflict; but there was never any necessity for the Union to set up the classical device for repressing an antagonistic population, which is a chain of fortified posts, with heavy patrols working among them, and stern reprisal against anyone who moves without official order.

The Union held the rivers. Not only were the rivers the main roads, but they cut across all other roads. The potential guerrillas might get supplies and even arms from speculators, but they were islanded by the tinclads, moving blockhouses which imposed none of the burdens of an army of occupation. It is not too much to say that if the breakthrough of the Mississippi barrier was strategically decisive of the large issue in the west, the gunboat patrols were quite as decisive of the small issue, so diffuse that its importance was concealed.

# 11

## Red River Valley

THE OVER-ALL STRATEGIC PLAN adumbrated by Grant when he was made lieutenant general and placed in charge of all the armies included an offensive by Banks overland from New Orleans against Mobile. A consideration of political strategy intervened; the troops of the French Empire were in Mexico, and Mr. Secretary Seward was fearful that they might support the independence of Texas or even demand its return. It was therefore "important that we immediately occupy some point or points in Texas" to show we still owned it, and this could best be done by an advance up the Red River, a program that would have the added advantages of opening up the sugar and cotton lands of northwest Louisiana and bringing more of that state under the administration of the newly organized loyalist government.

Banks had a mobile force of 10,000. General Sherman,

now commander of the west, agreed to lend Whisky Smith's division of 10,000 for the expedition, providing he got it back in time for his own campaign against Atlanta, which would begin in 30 days. Shreveport was to be the focal point; Steele of the Arkansas command would come overland to meet Banks there, while Porter convoyed the Marine Brigade, Smith's troops, and the supply up the stream, giving special attention to *Webb,* the last of the rebel rams.

The date of the expedition was more or less fixed by the peculiar water conditions in the river. It commonly begins to rise late in December, but really good boating is seldom attained before March, when it becomes possible for large steamers to pass the two sets of rapids over jagged rocks that are called the Falls of Alexandria. Porter chose the pick of his fleet: *Essex* (Commander Robert Townsend), *Benton* (Lieutenant Commander James A. Greer), *Lafayette* (Lieutenant Commander James P. Foster), *Choctaw* (Lieutenant Commander F. M. Ramsay), *Chillicothe* (Lieutenant J. P. Couthouy), *Louisville* (Lieutenant Commander E. K. Owen), *Carondelet* (Master James C. Gipson), *Eastport* (Lieutenant Commander S. L. Phelps), *Pittsburg* (Lieutenant W. R. Hoel), *Mound City* (Lieutenant Commander Byron Wilson), *Lexington* (Lieutenant G. M. Bache), with the tinclads *Ouachita* (Ensign Eugene Zimmerman), *Fort Hindman* (her name had been changed back to its original form) (Lieutenant John Pearce), *Cricket* (Master H. H. Gorringe), *Juliet* (Master John S. Watson), *Gazelle,* and the flagship *Black Hawk.* There were also the three new river monitors, queer-looking craft with a single turret bearing 2 11-inch guns and a hump in the afterdeck enclosing the wheel—*Ozark* (Lieutenant George W. Brown), *Neosho* (Lieutenant Samuel Howard) and *Osage,* the last under Selfridge.

He had been intended to take part in the expedition in *Conestoga,* but on the night of March 8, while she was coming downstream and therefore had the right of way under Mississippi rules, the officer of the deck of *General Price,* coming up, suddenly decided to cross her bows. He failed to make it; *General Price* drove her ram deep into *Conestoga's* side and the old timberclad sank in less than four minutes. Selfridge had been aboard *Cumberland* when she went down in Hampton Roads, besides having lost *Cairo;* when he reported this new sinking to Porter the latter only said: "Well, Selfridge, you do not seem to have much luck with the top of the alphabet. I think that for your next ship I will try the bottom."

On March 10 the naval vessels met at the mouth of the Red, with Smith's men on transports. The admiral was glad to see his old friend but took no good augury from the state of the water, uncommonly low for this time of year. About eight miles below Fort De Russy, which the Confederates had rebuilt, obstructions were encountered, lines of heavy piles braced together and helped out by a perfect forest of logs floated down from above. The troops were landed, while the gunboats went to work on the obstruction by pulling up the piles nearest the banks, which set up a rush of water to carry out the logs. The ironclads reduced the remaining piles by ramming. It was so slow a business and Smith had to bridge so many bayous that the Confederates made good their escape from the fort before either gunboats or troops could shut them in.

Porter now sent Phelps with *Eastport* on ahead to Alexandria to meet Banks' troops and to capture whatever

Confederate shipping there was in the river, but he only arrived on March 15, too late to get anything but the ruins of a burning steamer. Banks did not come until March 25, himself by water in the army *Black Hawk,* from which there debarked a whole regiment of cotton speculators, bearing licenses from Washington, the best recommended being those of the firm of (General Ben) Butler & Casey. An unstated strategic purpose of the campaign now appeared. Everybody was buying cotton or trying to get the navy to condemn it as property of the rebels, so they could pick it up cheaply in the prize courts. The coal barges were denuded of their cargo to make room for cotton; Breese and Selfridge were pestered daily to have cotton carried to Cairo; Lieutenant Dominy, on patrol at the mouth of the river, was offered another stripe if he would let the cotton through and dismissal if he did not.

Neither Porter nor Whisky Smith thought highly of these proceedings, and the latter had to hear his men described scornfully as "a bunch of ragged guerillas" by Banks. That officer was comfortably ensconced in a hotel, holding elections in the neighborhood; he seemed uninterested in the military campaign and the water was not rising satisfactorily. Smallpox broke out in the Marine Brigade, its hospital ship was wrecked, and its men became so nearly mutinous that they had to be sent back to Vicksburg. But at last, at the turn of the month, Banks got under way and the gunboats crawled through the Falls of Alexandria and moved up to Grand Ecore, where there is another set of rapids. They began to find burned cotton in vast quantities, but there was as yet no sign of resistance.

Except for *Eastport* the big ironclads were left below Grand Ecore, since above that point the Red winds around curves so violent that only with difficulty could any ships

be brought through. The army took a course across country while these bends were being negotiated, and an arrangement was made to meet at a point named Springfield
Landing, 40 miles below Shreveport. When Porter reached
that place, neither Banks nor any word from him was
there, and there was a new obstruction in the form of a
big steamer placed broadside across the stream, filled with
mud and then broken in the center. As Porter was con-
sidering how to deal with this obstacle, word at last came
from Banks; he had been heavily defeated at Sabine Cross
Roads, had lost all his supply train, and was in full retreat.
At the same time, instead of rising, the river began to fall.

## II

This instantly changed the position from difficult to
somewhere near desperate, for Porter was encumbered
with a number of large transports that had been brought
upstream in defiance of his orders. All had to go down
around all those bends, while the rebels could move across
country and make excellent practice with their artillery
from the high banks. There were numerous small snipings,
beginning at once, but the first real clash came on April 12
at a place called Blair's Landing, where two of the transports ran aground and General Tom Green attacked with
some 5000 Confederates. *Lexington* and *Osage* were the
escort, the latter with Banks' *Black Hawk* lashed to her
to help her around the turns. The two warships got a
crossfire on the advancing rebels and one of them blew
General Green's head off with a shell, but it was very
hot work indeed. All *Osage's* wooden outworks were destroyed by bullets and *Black Hawk* was so riddled that
there was not a spot on her six inches square that failed
to receive a hit. Several hundred Confederates were killed;

when the sailors climbed the banks after the enemy had been driven off, it was found that all their canteens smelled powerfully of Louisiana rum, which helps explain why they came on so hotly.

At Grand Ecore on the 15th, Porter found Banks, who closed a book, took off his glasses, and said he had been interrupted in the most pleasant occupation of his life: the reading of Scott's *Tactics*. Porter ground his teeth, but not audibly, and sought tidings. They were dismal. Whisky Smith and his ragged guerrillas had stopped the Confederates sharply at Pleasant Hill a few days after the first defeat, but Banks would not even let him collect his wounded, and, in spite of assuring Porter of his cooperation, was all for retreating downstream as fast as ever he could. Porter implored the general not to sacrifice the ships; the water was still falling, and if the army abandoned them above the rapids they were gone. The big *Eastport,* indeed, had to take her guns out to be dragged through at Grand Ecore. Banks' only answer to the appeal was to remark that the disaster at Sabine Cross Roads had been canceled by the repulse of the rebels at Pleasant Hill. His retreat order stood; Smith tried to get Franklin, the other division commander, to join him in removing Banks for incompetence; and discipline had to be tightened throughout the force to prevent a mutiny.

Now bad luck descended on *Eastport;* eight miles below the rapid a torpedo exploded under her bow. Porter was getting the lighter ships through when he heard the news. He boarded *Cricket* for a fast run down to Alexandria to get a pump boat to save *Eastport,* and ordered the heavy Pook turtles out of the falling river, they to send enough tinclads in from the Mississippi patrols as replacements. Two pump boats came back with the admiral; they could

not find *Eastport's* leak, but bulkheads were built to con-
fine it and, with the help of the pump boats, she staggered
on down. Just as the news that Banks had abandoned
Grand Ecore arrived, *Eastport's* keel jammed on a bed of
sunken logs, she could not be stirred from them and, with
the Confederates already sniping from the banks, had to
be abandoned. Powder was packed around her machinery
and trains of cotton and tar laid to her magazine. Porter
fired the trains himself and barely made his boat before
she blew.

This was on April 26. At this date there remained above
Alexandria only the two pump boats, crowded with Negro
refugees, *Juliet, Fort Hindman,* and the little *Cricket,*
which the rebels had attempted to board from the banks
while *Eastport* was being dealt with. But from the point
of her destruction down to Alexandria the road diverges
from the river and the ships had not even the support of
the retreating army. Porter aboard *Cricket* observed running around on a high bluff over a bend ahead and ordered
fire from the forward howitzer. At almost the same moment a terrific burst of shell from at least 18 concealed
heavy guns dropped on and around her and *Juliet,* and
both were raked with musketry. The admiral ran up to
the pilothouse just as one pilot was wounded; *Cricket*
had ceased fire and her engines were stopped; she was
drifting with the four-knot current. Porter ran back down
to the gundeck and found all the guns but one disabled;
in the fire room all the firemen were down and the engineer had been killed with his hand on the throttle, turning
it off. The admiral hastily organized reserve gun crews
and firemen from among the contrabands aboard and
hurried back topside, just as the second pilot was cut in
two by a shell. The little tinclad swirled around the point

of land, luckily to a position where she could enfilade the batteries and bring this business to a halt. In four minutes she had taken 38 hits and had 12 killed and 19 wounded in a crew of 50.

*Juliet* was nearly as badly hurt, with 15 casualties, but got under a bank and managed to turn back upstream. One of the pump boats was sunk; the rebels killed all the Negroes in the water. Above the batteries, Phelps aboard *Fort Hindman* could not but assume that *Cricket* and the admiral were gone; it was already falling dark over an uncertain channel with the sunken pump boat in the way, so he decided to wait for morning. At daybreak he ran through, comparatively little damaged because the Confederates were so interested in sinking the other pump boat and in killing the rest of their runaway slaves, something they succeeded in doing to their own satisfaction.

*Cricket,* meanwhile, had gone aground and was trying to put out a fire set by the enemy's shells. Porter got the fire under and the ship loose just about dark and she ran down, meeting Selfridge in *Osage* just coming up. He had been fighting another battery all day and, proof against their field guns, getting the best of it. The admiral sent him up for the other tinclads in the morning, but they had already passed the danger point.

### III

At Alexandria the ironclads were still above the Falls; had not been able to pass them on the low water. Banks was quartered comfortably in a hotel, with his troops camped around. He was voluble in his assurances that he would not abandon the fleet, but Porter had heard that sort of thing before and was advised that an officer had just arrived from Grant, demanding the return of Whisky

Smith's division. This meant that Banks would surely retreat again, no matter how hard he promised. The trouble was what to do about the ships. The Falls were in two groups, about a mile apart, with only a channel 20 feet wide and about three feet deep between, bare rocks showing on either side, and at least seven feet of water needed for the ironclads. Even the little *Cricket* only went through with much bumping and scraping; it was quite hopeless to expect that *Benton, Choctaw,* or *Chillicothe* could do it.

At this point appeared the *deus ex machina,* in the person of Colonel Joseph Bailey of the 4th Wisconsin, engineer officer on Franklin's staff, sent to Porter by that general. He was a lumberman; when a similar problem arose in his country about floating logs down a shallow stream, he said, they built wing dams to raise the water and carried everything through with a rush. He did not think it would be so very different with ships. Try it, try anything, said Porter, and went to Banks to get a detail of troops for the work.

After some persuasion Banks agreed to send 3000 men from Maine and New York regiments. They were by no means all lumberjacks[1] but they knew how to work. Bailey started at the lower Falls, where the stream is over 700 feet across. On the northern bank timber was plentiful; the trees were snaked to the river where men working to their waists in water placed them with roots upstream, cross-tying them with beams from all the plantation houses and cotton mills in the neighborhood. On the opposite side the trees had given way to plantations; the dam that sprang from this bank was made of heavy cribs filled with

[1] 29th Maine, 116th, 133rd, and 161st New York; one of them was from New York City.

stone, brick from torn-down houses, and fragments of iron. All the forges in the fleet made iron bolts to hold the cribs together; the seamen labored unceasingly at taking the armor off the ironclads and hoisting out their broadside guns. At the center the gap between the two wing dams was closed by three large barges, weighted with stone and sunk in the channel. It was planned that when the rising water had reached sufficient depth all the ships should run the upper Falls down to the barges, which would then be withdrawn for the second run.

By May 8 the flood was high enough for *Fort Hindman, Osage,* and *Neosho* to try running down and orders were given for the next morning. Before they could do it, the gathering waters swept aside the barges, and Bailey's lake began to sink visibly as the river gushed through the gap. Porter, his legs swollen with rheumatism, leaped on a horse, rode to the upper Falls, and ordered *Lexington,* as the oldest and least valuable ship, to try going all the way through. She went charging down the stream, pitched, rolled twice, bumped the barges in the wings, and stood on into deep water, while along the banks the soldier spectators burst into frantic cheering. *Neosho* followed to the lower gap; her pilot grew frightened and stopped his engines instead of giving them full steam, so that her hull was for a moment under water; but she too rode it out and was followed by *Fort Hindman* and *Osage.*

The other ironclads were still above, however, the water falling again, and Banks writing a letter to Porter, saying the game was up and he must leave. Privately (it was reported to the admiral) Banks told people that all the ships in the fleet were not worth a day's rations for his army. The two men hated each other all the rest of their lives, but what mattered most at the moment was that

Bailey was not in the least discouraged and promptly began building new wing dams at the upper Falls. Incredibly,
it took him just three days; on the 11th three of the ships
came through the upper Falls, and on the following day
the rest, all being helped by gangs hauling ropes from
the banks because of the crookedness of the channel. Below
they battened down hatches and took the plunge, all safely:
Porter had his ships back again. It was just in time; Banks
began his retreat even before *Ozark,* the last of them,
went through. There was some apprehension about the
lower bars, but the Mississippi was exceptionally full that
spring, and the back-up into the Red easily carried everything down.

The news that met the admiral below Alexandria was
not of a character to make him feel any better about political generals. McClernand, the marplot of the Vicksburg
campaign, had turned up again, in charge of Banks' communications. He picked up enough cotton to fill a large
steamer, and demanded convoy down the Red. On May 4
Porter assigned to him *Signal* and *Covington,* the two best
tinclads below the Falls, under command of Lieutenant
G. P. Lord. Next morning a rebel force with artillery got
past McClernand and attacked all; the river was so low
and the banks so high that the tinclads' guns could not
reach and both were soon cut to pieces. Lord managed
to get *Covington* into the bank, burn her, and escape with
31 of his 76 men; *Signal* had to be surrendered and was
sunk by the Confederates.

So the war's last river campaign came to a dismal end.
Whose fault? Clearly Banks' at the point of contact. Few
generals ever did anything so silly as to keep the train
with the vanguard, as he did at Sabine Cross Roads; few
ever showed less spirit than he did at Pleasant Hill, where

200 CIVIL WAR ON WESTERN WATERS

he retreated after beating off the enemy; few ever did anything like his abandonment of the fleet. But behind this failure of Banks there is something to be said about the part Washington played. They knew what kind of a general he was; and his appointment to New Orleans was made at least partly to give him an administrative command where he would not have to do any fighting. Also, he could always plead with a certain amount of justice that the 30-day restriction on the use of A. J. Smith's division hopelessly hamstrung the operation. The whole campaign stinks of military considerations subordinated to politics.

Yet over and around all this rises the fact that amphibious operations were carried into a country beyond their reach. If Banks had reached Shreveport and fortified himself there, his communications must have come by water and in the low summer river they could not have been kept up. It was lucky for his army that it retreated when it did. Alexandria was the last point that could really be supported by ships; there was only trouble above, as the attack on *Cricket* showed.

# 12

# Small War Revived— and Ended

Dᴜʀɪɴɢ 1863 it was gradually borne in upon Confederate raiders along the rivers that without artillery it was not profitable to attack anything under tinclad protection. The results of this lesson became increasingly apparent as the year turned into 1864 and the war of mobile cavalry units against river posts and traffic opened out again if, indeed, it can ever be said to have ceased. Railroads in the South were in a state of wreck and even the shipments that had not previously gone by water were being driven to the rivers. But in Georgia, Sherman was drawing in every man he could get for the big campaign against Atlanta, the river posts were mostly small and largely held by Negro troops. The very idea such troops existed was an intolerable insult to the South; it was always easy to assemble men on horseback to join the regular cavalry and the guns for an attack on such a post.

Quite typical were the events at Waterproof, Louisiana, on February 13. The place was an inconsiderable hamlet south of Vicksburg, where a receiving depot had been set up for the collection of Negroes and cattle, with 280 colored troops in garrison, and *Forest Rose* (Lieutenant L. V. Johnston) was in the river. On the afternoon of the 13th a force estimated by the defenders as 800 cavalry, but probably less, twice tried to storm the place; a good many of the colored soldiers panicked and it was only the shells from the tinclad that saved the situation. Lieutenant Commander James A. Greer, in charge of the area, heard the firing upstream and arrived that night with *Rattler*. The two naval men agreed that the show was not over and Greer went down to Natchez for reinforcements. Before he could get back the rebels tried again, now with some infantry and four guns in support of their cavalry. *Forest Rose* had been equipped with a couple of Parrott rifles in addition to her howitzers (they had been found best for dealing with shore artillery and many of the ships now had them); they were altogether too much for the enemy fieldpieces, while the howitzers took care of the rest. Johnston got a strictly unusual letter of commendation from the army man in charge.

Arkansas was in Union hands at least to the line of the Washita, but there were considerable, loosely organized, Confederate forces along that river and it was not strategically worthwhile sending an expedition powerful enough to dislodge them. Porter thought they might be shaken up by a gunboat raid, and on February 29 Lieutenant Commander Frank M. Ramsay started up the winding Black with *Fort Hindman* (Pearce), *Ouachita* (Byron Wilson), *Lexington* (Bache), *Conestoga* (Selfridge), *Cricket* (Gorringe), and the monitor *Osage* (Master Thomas Wright). This was not a prelude to the Red River campaign, on which discussions had only begun the day after the expedition left. The objective was rebel forts and concentrations, of which nothing serious was encountered till March 2 at Harrisonburg, where a brigade of sharpshooters opened fire from behind the levee and a battery of 12-pounders joined in. *Osage* had just suffered a breakdown in the main wheel of her turret; it would not turn, and the flagship *Fort Hindman* had to carry most of the load. She was hit 27 times and her starboard engine disabled, but the other ships got below a bend, enfiladed the levee, and drove off battery and sharpshooters with many dead. Ramsay pushed on a little farther, but the river was low and falling, so he turned back. Harrisonburg he burned; some guns found nearby were carried off. Porter expressed himself as perfectly satisfied with the results.

On March 9, the same day Ramsay's squadron reached the rallying point at the mouth of the Red, there was a fight at Yazoo City, which had been occupied in February by 1100 troops supported by the tinclads *Petrel* (Master Thomas McElroy) and *Marmora* (Master Gibson). The Confederates stormed the place with two brigades, 2000 men, and, though they could not take a redoubt in the outskirts, broke into the town. A fierce little street fight blazed up. The only piece of artillery ashore was disabled by a jammed shot; McElroy sent a howitzer and crew under an ensign from his ship, Shepley R. Holmes, while the soldiers rolled bales of cotton to make a barricade. At the first fire Holmes and his men ran away back to the ship; the infantry ashore manned the piece and, helped by the gunboats, drove off the Confederate forces after some six hours of fighting that dwindled down to desultory sniping. Losses on both sides were about ten per cent of those engaged, which means that the really hot work did not last long.

There was a somewhat similar affair at Paducah, Kentucky, on March 25, part of Cavalry Forrest's long, heavy raid up the alley between the Mississippi and Tennessee. Shirk, who was in command of the section of the Ohio that includes Paducah, arrived at the town to find that Colonel S. G. Hicks, who commanded the fort and place with 800 Negro recruits, was nervous about attack. The naval man had heard this sort of thing so frequently that he expressed some skepticism; nevertheless he left behind his own ship, the tinclad *Peosta* (Lieutenant Thomas E. Smith), and took a dispatch boat down to Cairo, where he had business. *Paw Paw* (Lieutenant A. B. O'Neill) was also on station. Shirk was hardly out of sight when, a little after three in the afternoon, the rebels appeared and tried to rush the fort with about 5000 men. *Peosta* had the exceptionally heavy armament of 3 30-pound rifles and 3 32-pounders in addition to the usual six howitzers; she and *Paw Paw* put out more fire than Forrest's men could stand. They left off direct attack and began an approach through the town, setting up a terrific rifle fire from windows against the tinclads to keep them out of it. This failed; Smith shelled the buildings, demolishing the City Hotel and the brewery and setting several other structures afire, but it was nearly midnight when Forrest drew off, having lost some 300 killed, including one of his brigadiers.

It may have been this setback at a post held by Negroes that accounts for the singular barbarity with which Forrest's men behaved at Fort Pillow, on April 12, a little over two weeks later. There was a tinclad present, *New Era* (Master James Marshall), but she was one of the smallest and weakest of the class, only 157 tons, and with a strong wind blowing and current running, could give little help fighting with head downstream. The place was taken and most of those inside shot down in cold blood, while its guns were turned on *New Era* and drove her off. It was the only post with gunboat support taken during the war.

The post at Yazoo City had been intended only as a support to Sherman's winter Meridian expedition and was given up after the attack on it as not worth the trouble of maintenance; but in April someone got the idea that there might be some cotton around there, and an expedition was organized to collect it. Colonel Hiram Scofield had a force to march overland from Haines' Bluff; Navy was asked to cooperate and sent *Petrel* (McElroy) and *Prairie Bird* (Ensign J. W. Chalmers). On April 21 the ships moved up: *Prairie Bird* was hit by the fort, partially disabled, and had to stay below, but *Petrel* got through. Next morning, above the fort, in a stretch of river so narrow that he could not turn round, with no sign of *Prairie Bird* or Scofield, McElroy began to feel anxious. He had good reason; as he was getting up from table after a noon dinner, rifled guns suddenly opened up from the underbrush, the very first shot cutting the steampipe, while a perfect hail of musketry was aimed at the gunports, making firing slow from the difficulty of loading. Another shot struck *Petrel's* boiler and the same Ensign Holmes who ran away at Yazoo City before leaped to the bank and raced off through the fields, followed by most of the crew. The Confederates took and burned *Petrel,* which prevented McElroy from receiving a note written that morning by Scofield, whom he was supposed to be supporting: "It was not deemed prudent to move the land forces to Yazoo City." As for Holmes, he was placed under arrest when he reached Vicksburg and dismissed the service for scandalous conduct.

The Confederates tried their new technique of firing suddenly from concealed batteries on the Mississippi also, on June 1, when the tinclad *Exchange* (Master James C. Gipson) was coming upstream near Columbia, a town now vanished. The ship had just rounded a sand bar on a curve when she was suddenly assailed by a crossfire from batteries below and above, nine guns all told, hidden behind the levee. The accepted remedy in such a case is to back down, but the sand bar prevented; Gipson had to take his ship on upstream, returning the fire as best he could. The port engine was disabled, and it was only by some pretty smart work on the part of the engineers that *Exchange* won past with 35 shots through her, badly crippled.

The area was one of heavy traffic; everything was immediately placed under convoy, the ram *Monarch* taking two ships through, while another went up in care of Owen's *Louisville*. Both were fired on; the rifled shell came right through *Louisville's* unarmored aftersection and wounded five men, and the transport covered by *Monarch* was hit 28 times. Owen, who was in naval command of that section of the stream, reported that he could convoy all right, but with "the usual loss of men and injury to boats"; a military expedition was necessary. It was made on June 5 by that old friend of the gunboats, Whisky Smith, who summarily disposed of the opposition after two days of light fighting.

The thing was tried next on June 8, near Simmesport,

on the Atchalfaya, that strange stream which is half-lagoon and half-river. Lieutenant Commander Frank Ramsay had intelligence of the rebels doing something there and went down for a look with *Chillicothe, Neosho,* and *Fort Hindman.* They were there, two 30-pounder rifles, which opened immediately. It was an almost bloodless battle; the Parrotts could not get through the armor of the ironclads and although most of their shells missed (the Confederates reported a casualty list of three), they drove off the gunners and their infantry support and landed a party which captured the guns.

Just a week later another battery attacked *General Bragg* (Dominy) while she was at anchor off Como Landing near Port Hudson. She soon put it out of business, but at one-forty-five in the morning it came back and was lucky enough to hit *General Bragg's* walking beam, so that she drifted down the stream, disabled, and had to be helped out by the monitor *Winnebago,* which presently appeared. The report of Colonel J. S. Scott, the Confederate officer commanding the guns, gives a great deal of illumination; he tells how he moved the pieces from place to place until the monitor took a hand and: "I have little hesitation in saying that with guns of a proper caliber, gunboats can be made very scarce, particularly tinclads."

For his part Porter also wanted something he did not have. "These batteries," he reported, "will continue to come in on the river until more effective measures are taken by the military authorities to land troops and chase them up." He was almost through with the river assignment; as early as May he had been summoned East for a spot of leave and talks with the Department, which were to result in his taking over the North Atlantic blockading squadron with the special mission of organizing an attack on the great stronghold of Fort Fisher. The admiral delayed as long as possible; not only was he genuinely sorry to leave the river command, but he wanted this matter of the flying batteries cleared up and, above all, a series of measures to control the smuggling that occupied more of his time than anything else. He had now divided the rivers into 11 districts, with an officer in charge of each, full responsibility for everything that went on in his area. On July 3 he finally and reluctantly took his departure, leaving the perfect trump Pennock in charge and hoping that he had placed things in tolerable order.

Well, at least on the Mississippi he had. During all the rest of the war there was only one other battery incident of record on the main stream, in August, when some field-pieces suddenly opened on the commercial steamer *Empress* near Waterproof, killing her captain and several of her people. *Prairie Bird* and *Romeo* were on patrol and soon disposed of the battery.

The proximate reason why this cessation of antinaval activity on the Mississippi took place so suddenly after the June attacks lies forever lost in those records that Judah P. Benjamin had burned at the fall of Richmond. The long-range, basic reason can be found in reverse in the Scott report—guns "of a proper caliber." Even when rifles, the 9-, 10-, and 12-pound mobile fieldpieces could not stand up against the 24- and 30-pounders on the ships, and when the Confederates tried using heavier artillery, as at Simmesport, ironclads put in an appearance and the shore guns could neither match them nor escape.

## II

Yet if the fighting on the Mississippi was over, there was still to unroll there one of the most singular transactions of the war. On September 4 the old *Rattler,* one of the first and most active of the tinclads, was patrolling near the mouth of the Red, commanded by a master named Daniel W. Glenney, who had been the mate of a clipper out of New York. That evening he remarked to the other officers that a Negro had told him that during the night there would be at the home of a Mr. James his two sons, Confederate officers, who would be worth the taking. The cutter was manned after dark and 22 men in charge of the assistant engineer were sent to the Louisiana shore to make the capture. A quarter of a mile in they were suddenly hailed from the dark and ordered to surrender, they were surrounded. There was a blaze of fire, a couple of men were hit, and there came a rush in which all but three of the *Rattlers* were overpowered and carried off prisoners.

Aboard the ship, skipper Glenney expressed himself as perturbed at the sound of firing, ordered out the dinghy with an armed crew under Ensign H. N. Wells, and stood slowly downstream. Current appears to have carried Wells and his dinghy in the same direction farther than he wished. The ensign made out the cutter pulling for the ship a little ahead of him, hailed, got an "Aye, aye" for an answer, and, not satisfied with that or with the accent in which it was given, asked the officer of the cutter his name. There was no answer; Wells fired his revolver and his men their muskets, whereupon the cutter turned back to shore.

Later in the night *Rattler* was hailed from the bank and the voice of the engineer who had been in charge of the landing party being recognized, he was taken aboard and told the story of what had happened. Next day Glenney left his ship and went upstream to report the event in person to Selfridge, who had command of the district. The latter was outraged; only a couple of weeks before Glenney had narrowly escaped capture on one of these shore expeditions and had been given positive orders not to let anyone go ashore beyond cover of the ship's guns. Selfridge told Glenney to return to his command; instead the master went on up to Vicksburg, telling the garrison commander there that he was on parole, but still in command of the ship, and that his parole required him not to use her guns on the enemy.

This seemed so singular to the general that he made a report to Selfridge, who put Glenney under hack, confined to his ship, and himself sent in a report asking for the master's dismissal. But on October 24 a rebel deserter came off to *Benton,* also in the area, with a story that complicated matters. On the occasion when Glenney had been so nearly captured, he had really been getting in touch with the Confederate command, had offered to arrange for the capture of *Rattler* in exchange for $2000 and 100 bales of cotton, and had been taken up on it. The men who ambushed the cutter's crew were from the Confederate ironclad *Missouri,* building up the Red; they intended to board the tinclad, and only the accident of the current drift and Wells' alertness had kept them from it, since at the crucial moment nearly three quarters of the ship's crew were out of her.

As Selfridge remarked, this was hearsay, but it fitted all the circumstances extremely well, including the fact that when he reached Vicksburg, Glenney was unusually flush. Selfridge had him placed in close arrest aboard *Rattler,* with a sentry at the door. There presently arrived from *Benton* a letter which Glenney had given to one of her officers for mailing (something he had no right to do while under hack) and which the officer had turned in to his captain. It was addressed to a girl in Mississippi and contained an interesting passage:

The insult that has been put upon me by the servant of an imbecile Government has sunk deep into my heart. I now live for one purpose, and that is deep, bitter revenge. Like a snake I will sting when least expected and my name shall be a terror to every Yankee. The haunts of old ocean are too familiar to me to fear their fast cruisers. There are other brave hearts that will sail under my orders who are now serving under the Federal Government.

This was a piece of conviction; preparations for a trial were made, though without too much attention to that final sentence. But on the night of November 3 Ensign E. P. Nellis relieved the deck aboard *Rattler* and when the morning of November 4 came both he and Glenney had disappeared and so had the skiff that hung from the paddle guard. Neither of them was ever found.

### III

On the tributary rivers things were different; the ships had more difficulty in moving and every time an organized force approached one of the streams there would be clashes with its cavalry. In June, General Frederick Steele, commanding at Little Rock, desired to extend his right wing farther up the Arkansas and asked Ledyard Phelps, the district naval commander, to convoy his transports down the White from Devall's Bluff and thence up the Arkansas. Phelps referred the request to Porter; Porter told him to furnish the convoy if he thought the water up the Arkansas high enough. Phelps didn't but, rather than give the army any cause of complaint about cooperation, ordered *Tyler*,

*Naumkeag,* and *Fawn* up the White under Lieutenant Commander G. M. Bache. At this date the last two, with *Queen City,* were between Clarendon and St. Charles; *Lexington* (temporarily Ensign Henry Booby) was at White River Station, the mouth of the White.

Before the ships could do more than get their orders, word ran in that General Joseph Orville Shelby had anticipated Steele's move by getting clear around that right wing with 2500 raiding cavalry and five guns, and was coming down the left bank of the White. First contact was on June 22 by *Lexington* at White River Station, where 56 men of the 12th Iowa in a stockade were rushed by a wing of 300 Confederate cavalry; the ship drove them off.

Two days later Shelby himself spotted *Queen City* (Master Michael Hickey) near Clarendon and decided to try the night-surprise game on him; between three and four in the morning guns opened from the dark at the tinclad, getting hits in the engines at once. It was *Petrel* over again; two of Hickey's ensigns panicked; he could make no effective return to the enemy fire; and he told his people they could choose between trying to swim for it and being prisoners, he was going to surrender.

Bache was upstream with *Tyler, Naumkeag,* and *Fawn,* having just picked up the transports. At nine in the morning, on the way down, he got news of the *Queen City* disaster and, hoping at least to save the ship's equipment, sent the transports back up and hurried on with his warships. Before he got there Shelby blew the ship up, but his troops were disposed around the bend where they had taken her when the gunboats arrived and he decided to make a fight of it. The result was the usual one between field batteries and gunboats; *Tyler* got below the Confederates while the other two vessels remained above, giving the troops a crossfire. "Finding I could do no more damage, I withdrew a distance of two miles," reported Shelby, not adding that he left one of his guns and most of his dead behind. The transports never did get convoyed down the White.

## IV

On September 3 Slocum's corps of Sherman marched into the streets of Atlanta. Confederate Hood circled, swung west into Alabama, and turned north toward Tennessee, with some idea of forcing Sherman to loose his grip on Georgia; Forrest, still operating south and west of the Tennessee River, would fall in on him as a cavalry wing. As he came north naval operations blazed up again; it was important to give General Thomas at Nashville as much time as possible to pull his patchwork army together, and the river line, striking across Alabama, was the best place for delaying action. The first event in the new campaign was a wire from Sherman himself on October 10 to Lieutenant H. A. Glassford, commanding the upper Tennessee; Hood should be "prevented from crossing the Tennessee anywhere above Mussel Shoals." That is, kept away from east Tennessee and Chattanooga.

There were now ships above Mussel Shoals, four of extremely light draft built at Chattanooga by Army, *General Burnside, General Grant, General Sherman, General Thomas*, operationally under Navy, armed with a pair of 20-pound rifles and three or four howitzers apiece.

The day of Sherman's telegram there was action at Eastport, still held by the Confederates, whom it was desirable to dispossess. An expedition of three small regiments and a battery of artillery was sent against the place in three transports under convoy of the tinclads *Undine*

(Lieutenant E. M. King) and *Key West*. As the troops were just debarking, masked batteries of six and three rifled guns opened a crossfire on the whole group. Two of the transports were hit at once, disabled, and set afire by exploding ammunition; as they went drifting away the troops on the river bank broke and abandoned their guns. *Undine* and *Key West* maintained the contest for 30 minutes but they had only smoothbores, which could accomplish nothing against the rifles ashore and, after collecting all the stragglers they could, they pulled out.

The report of this affair brought another telegram from Sherman to Thomas: "Order in my name renewal of the attempt to get Eastport, and ask Admiral Porter to send up an ironclad." (Sherman did not know it, but it was no longer his friend Porter he was addressing; Porter had received his definite orders to the North Atlantic, and the man he replaced there, S. Phillips Lee, had been given the river command, principally to show there was no positive disapproval of anything he had done. He was a relative of the Lees of Virginia, but in a collateral line.) Greer, commanding the area, replied from Mound City that there was not water enough in the river for any ironclad, but he was ordering more tinclads in, and would attempt Eastport again as soon as there were troops to cooperate.

Lieutenant Moreau Forrest, who had relieved Glassford in command of the four *Generals,* was meanwhile ordered to bring them down from Bridgeport to the region just above Decatur, where the Confederates were showing signs of activity. There is a bar at Bridgeport and only *General Thomas* (Master Gilbert Morton) was below it; the water was so low that efforts to jump the others over failed. But *General Thomas* arrived at Decatur with a small army gunboat on October 28, just as Hood's vanguard tried to win a crossing under cover of artillery; the two drove out the Confederate batteries in a sharp little action in which both gunboats were a good deal cut up. Hood was driven westward, with the required immunity to Chattanooga and the required delay, and had to make his crossing just below the Shoals, at Tuscumbia-Florence.

Meanwhile Confederate Forrest had been strengthened, was raiding energetically up the Tennessee and demonstrating that he had fully learned about the use of light rifled artillery by surprise. Supply ships could not move along the river without convoy and several of them were caught and burned out during those fading days of October. On the 30th the rebels trapped *Undine* (Master J. L. Bryant) about 50 miles above Paducah and just below Johnsonville. A battery of seven guns put a crossfire on her; her furnace was hit and the fires put out, a steam pipe severed; the ship was gradually being knocked to pieces when her commander ran her into the east bank, struck his flag, and got away with as many of his men as he could, overland to Fort Donelson. The transport *Venus,* which came down without answering Bryant's signals to go back, was also taken.

Shirk, commanding the upstream district and Fitch, commanding that downstream, moved in to see about this plague spot. They found a wide island, Reynoldsburg Island, which compressed the river to a narrow chute with a highly irregular channel and a curve. The batteries were all along this curve and at the ends of it, so placed that any ship coming up must expose her stern to some of them without reply. It later developed that the Confederates now had about 15 guns in position, all rifles, but this was not known when on November 4 the double attack was was made, Lieutenant E. M. King taking *Key West, Tawah*

(Lieutenant Williams), and *Elfin* (Master A. F. Thompson) in from upstream, Fitch himself bringing *Moose, Paw Paw,* and *Fairy* in from below. The first move was a success; King recaptured the transport *Venus* and fired so heavily into *Undine,* now under Confederate occupation, that the rebels burned her.

But now came action against the batteries and things began to go wrong. *Tawah* was a new boat, hastily equipped; most of her shells would not fit the guns. The shells from the rifled artillery ashore went through and through the ships, *Key West's* stern-wheel was fouled by her cable and all three pretty much disabled, with guns and engines out of operation and ammunition nearly gone. They could only drift, farther down under the batteries. "With a heavy heart" King gave orders to run the ships ashore and burn them with seven transports, an act for which he was later censured. He and his men marched to Johnsonville to join the garrison and help hold the place against the Confederates. He reported that nothing would make the river secure but a large land force with ironclads. It was the stiffest setback the river navy had taken; at Donelson and Grand Gulf no ships were lost.

Thomas also asked for ironclads, and *Carondelet* and *Neosho* were ordered to Paducah, to ascend the Tennessee as soon as the fall rains produced enough water to float them. But Forrest was more interested in making trouble than in effecting a lodgment on the Tennessee. He sent some of his men across the river, who began to work toward the Cumberland, while the general himself operated up the old corridor between Mississippi and Tennessee. Thomas was by this time achieving his concentration at Nashville, so that when the ironclads found enough water they went up the Cumberland under the general command of Fitch, with the tinclads *Brilliant, Fairplay, Moose, Reindeer,* and *Silver Lake.*

Hood closed Nashville during November and, under the impression he was besieging Thomas, flung out his left wing to Bell's Mills, on the river four miles below the city, and built a pair of shore batteries to command the stream. All the ships were then at Nashville; Fitch moved downstream on the night of December 3, with *Carondelet,* followed by *Fairplay* (Master George J. Groves), *Moose, Reindeer* (Lieutenant H. A. Glassford), and *Silver Lake* (Master J. C. Coyle). The plan was a reversal of the Confederate night surprises: *Carondelet* to slide silently downstream, rounding to just below the battery, with the others behind her in line, all firing suddenly from the dark.

It worked to perfection; the Confederates never saw the ships till they started shooting. Funnel and gun smoke soon settled so thick that Fitch in *Moose* at the center of the line, could see absolutely nothing. He had to back up to join *Reindeer* and *Silver Lake* above. The Confederate fire mostly went over, and the shells that did hit often failed to explode. After a good deal of passionate but futile musketry they gave up and in the morning the batteries were gone.

Later they came back and built new works, three batteries high on the hills. Fitch took *Neosho* (Lieutenant Samuel Howard) down on December 7 and had a single-handed duel with them, in which the monitor was hit 100 times without suffering any damage and the batteries probably did not sustain much more, high as they were. But by December 7 General Thomas had his plan and most of his equipment, waiting only on weather. He wanted those batteries to stay right where they were. The ships thus saw no more action until, on the night of the

14th, Fitch received a note saying he was to go down next morning, but to attract attention only. He led the way with *Neosho,* taking her down below the lowest battery; the tinclads opened a long-range, harmless duel with those above. This lasted till twilight, when there fell a silence on the hills and a silence on the ships; next morning Union cavalry guidons were waving where the batteries had stood and the guns were taken.

The war on western waters was over.

No more amphibious operations; no more dueling with batteries; no more convoys. It only remained to pick up the pieces. The first one fell into place on April 24, 1865, early on a hazy morning, when a ship ran down the Mississippi, bearing the lights of a transport. It struck Lieutenant William Willis of *General Price* that there was something peculiar about this vessel; she did not stop at the usual transport landing. He tried to telegraph New Orleans, but the line would not work; when he did get through he learned that she was indeed a suspicious character, the elusive ram *Webb,* last survivor of the Hollins squadron. With several vessels in pursuit, she reached a point 20 miles below New Orleans where, it being now broad daylight, the armed tug *Hollyhock* fired a broadside into her; she ran into the bank and was blown up.

She was not, however, the last survivor of the Confederate States river navy. That was the ironclad *Missouri,* built up the Red River, which never saw any action and was surrendered at the end of May. A surveying officer found: "She is a most formidable vessel," but: "She is badly built of green timber, caulked with cotton, leaks badly and is very slow. From all I can judge of her, I do not consider her of any use as an ironclad."

It might serve as an epitome and epitaph for the whole Confederate river navy.

## V

What does it add up to? What were the underlying causes of victory and defeat?

The usual answer is that the South suffered from a lack of material resources, and to a degree this is true. They had no Pittsburgh, they sheathed their armored ships in railroad iron, and there was constant difficulty with engines. It would have taken an extraordinary effort to overcome all this.

But to accept material shortages as the sole cause for the Confederate defeats on western waters is not merely to neglect analysis; it is also to reject the testimony of the Confederate leaders themselves. Rodgers encountered similar troubles when he went west to build the first gunboats, and if the Union commanders were better supplied mechanically, they always had trouble finding crews. The real key factors lay in the urgency, the purpose, the command, and the strategy.

No one on the Confederate side had the sense of time that drove Jim Eads. No one on that side achieved the concept that a naval war, even on a river, cannot be won by the defensive. Even after the highly successful attacks at the Head of Passes and Plum Point Bend the lesson was lost on the Confederate authorities.

They were locked in the strategic concept of Jefferson Davis, that of holding the river by means of forts, with the naval forces merely auxiliary. In contrast is the attitude of the Union commanders. They were there for attack, on land and water, whatever the means available, and if one branch of the assault failed, as at Donelson, the other might break through. It is hard to avoid the conclusion that the Confederate land forces might have accomplished something against Grant at Fort Henry while he was in the debarkation stage, or the Confederate naval forces have done something against Pope before *Carondelet* made her spectacular dash past Island No. 10, if in either case the commands had been coordinated by the idea of striking the enemy. The Federal forces worked as a team because they had this common idea; the Confederates waited to be struck and were destroyed in detail.

Defensive thinking is in the background of the most obvious and fatal of Confederate errors, divided command. Mansfield Lovell, Polk, Hollins, Montgomery, the Tifts, Isaac Brown, all had different ideas about how the river should be defended, and since from the distance of Richmond it appeared that these ideas complemented each other, all were adopted. In reality, instead of complementing, they competed. Polk thought he needed soldiers more than the yards needed carpenters and mechanics, and would not release the men from the army; Lovell, Hollins, and the Tifts wanted the same dockyard space, metal parts, and engines; the river ships were fatally divided between Memphis and New Orleans; and at both places they had to fight without any help from the army.

Thus, though very real, the shortages from which the Confederacy suffered were compounded by the Confederacy's own acts. By May, 1863, to be sure, no further acts on the river would have been adequate; Vicksburg was under siege and the building yards were gone; strategy on the rivers had ceased to be naval. But it was not the case earlier, when both sides started with nothing but some river steamers and ideas. What might have been accomplished on the Confederate side by unified command and unified application of the available resources and energies is a matter of speculation, but it is beyond speculation that Grant did achieve the substance of unified command and purpose with his naval commanders.

The outlook of the Confederate leaders was limited to their own immediate needs and desires, and this visibly ran back through all the stages into the design and construction of the ships. *Louisiana, Mississippi, Arkansas* were interesting and ingenious vessels, but none of them showed real coordination among the results to be produced, the materials available for production, and, above all, the time in which production had to be achieved. The old Pook turtles and the Ellet rams were nowhere near as good as any of the three Confederates, but they were ready when needed, and it was not solely because they were backed by better factory equipment.

The construction and operations of the Union river navy were throughout backed and informed by the liveliest sense that the duty of ships on inland waters was close cooperation with the forces ashore. Only in the single case when *Arkansas* was sent down to cooperate in the attack on Baton Rouge was there any similar effort on the Confederate side, and even in this case the commander ashore failed to inform himself of the state of the ship. The Confederate command afloat, already bound to an impossible defensive, already divided, was still farther bound and divided by the fact that it had almost no relations with the land forces. And after it was wiped out the Union armies operating along a river line always had one secure flank and, in spite of the troubles of the tinclads, communications that could not be attacked with effect.

# Notes on Bibliography

OF COURSE, the main reliance in preparing this work has been the *Official Records, Union and Confederate Navies,* a government publication. The men on the spot did not always see things correctly, nor report correctly what they saw, but they were better than anyone else. Since the campaigns on the rivers were amphibious, the *Official Records, Union and Confederate Armies* have also been laid under contribution.

Admiral Mahan wrote an excellent book called *The Gulf and Inland Waters* in the *Campaigns of the Civil War* series, and he had the benefit of personal contact with many of the participants. But he covered more ground in a much shorter work than this, and did not have the *Official Records,* the searching out and publication of which was not completed until 1922. His book also ranks as a major source.

So does Admiral D. D. Porter's *Naval History of the Civil War,* in spite of many inaccuracies, which have usually been checked through the *Official Records.* The big *Battles and Leaders of the Civil War,* published by Century in the 1880's, and written by the participants. *The Confidential Correspondence of G. V. Fox* falls in the same order of sources.

Of unpublished manuscript sources, very few were

utilized; there is still some unpublished Fox correspondence in the New York Historical Society Library and a
little material in National Archives, but the compilers of
the *Official Records* did such a good job that very little
was added from these sources.

Among quasi-contemporary sources, Scharf's *History
of the Confederate States Navy,* a hard book to find and
still harder to keep together when found, deserves mention; so does Boynton's *History of the Navy,* which deals
only with the Civil War and is marred by long passages of
rhetoric.

Of secondary sources there is a long list. H. Allen Gos-
nell's *Guns on the Western Waters* is an excellent job,
largely a compilation from contemporary accounts and
postwar memoirs, with some intercalary material as brac-
ing. Richard West, Jr., has written two excellent books,
full of research adequately expressed: *Gideon Welles* and
*The Second Admiral,* a biography of D. D. Porter. He
also did a useful article, "Relations Between Porter and
Farragut," *U. S. Naval Institute Proceedings,* July, 1935.
The Reverend Joseph T. Durkin, S.J., has an excellen :
*Stephen R. Mallory,* recently published and full of new
material. Prof. C. S. Lewis has written a *David Glasgow
Farragut* that outdoes all other biographies of its subject
and has been treated as the authoritative source wherever
there is conflict. W. J. Abbot's *Bluejackets of '61* has a
number of anecdotes given nowhere else and stands up
surprisingly well when tested for accuracy by original
sources.

Minor sources used comprise: How's *James B. Eads* and
Dorsey's *Road to the Sea,* two good, though sparse, biog-
raphies of the same man. The *Personal Memoirs of U. S.
Grant* of course was used. William H. Russell's *My Diary,*

*North and South* supplied interesting details. Over-all strategic and tactical considerations came from H. W. Wilson's *Battleships in Action* and D. W. Knox' *History of the Navy,* neither of which had space enough to give much detailed coverage.

Other minor sources are: *Official Correspondence Between the War Department and General Lovell* (Confederate), "Mansfield Lovell," by General G. W. Smith, in *Association of the Graduates of the U. S. Military Academy, Annual Reunion, 1884; Dictionary of American Biography;* F. V. Greene's *The Mississippi;* Pfisterer's *Statistical Record;* Cist's *Army of the Cumberland* (the last three all in the *Campaigns of the Civil War* series); *Memoirs of T. O. Selfridge;* Walke, *Naval Scenes and Reminiscences;* Rear Admiral W. W. Parks, "Building a War Ship in the Southern Confederacy" in *U. S. Naval Institute Proceedings,* August, 1923; *Missouri Historical Review,* Vol. XXV; Henry Cabot Lodge's *Early Memories;* Browne, *Four Years in Secessia;* Jim Dan Hill, *Sea Dogs of the Sixties* (for some interesting material on Farragut and Winslow); Gift, "Story of the *Arkansas,*" *Southern Historical Society Papers,* Vol. XII; Coleman, "A July morning with the Rebel Ram *Arkansas,*" *Loyal Legion, Commandery of the State of Michigan,* Vol. I; *Diary of Gideon Welles;* Porter's *Incidents and Anecdotes of the Civil War* (a damned bad book); Hammersley, *Records of Living Officers of the U. S. Navy and Marine Corps;* Eaton's *History of the Southern Confederacy.*

Much use was also made of contemporary newspaper and magazine accounts, especially those in *Leslie's* and *Harper's Weekly,* which had time to select from the items coming over the wire. Mention should also be made of J. F. Baxter's *Coming of the Ironclad Warship,* though this supplied only a few lines, and Bennett's *Steam Navy of the United States,* the same.

Footnotes to these sources have been consistently omitted, as being an obstruction to the reader. They stand in the original manuscript, and if anyone wishes to question the author by letter as to where he got authority for a given statement, he will be happy to reply.

# Appendix

## List of Confederate and Union Ships

### A. SHIPS OF THE CONFEDERATE RIVER NAVY

#### I. The Hollins Fleet

*Calhoun*—Purchased at New Orleans. Side-wheel steamer, 500 tons. Battery: 1 16-pounder, 2 12-pounders, 2 6-pounders. Burned after the fall of New Orleans.

*General Polk*—Purchased 1861. Battery: February, 1862, 6 guns. Burned in Yazoo River, June, 1862.

*Ivy*—Purchased late 1861. Side-wheel steamer, 454 tons. 191 feet long, 28 feet beam. Battery: January, 1862, 1 8-inch rifle, 2 24-pound howitzers. Burned in the Yazoo to avoid capture, 1863.

*Maurepas* (formerly *Grosse Tête*)—Purchased 1861. Battery: 5 guns, 32 and 24-pounders. Sunk in the White River, June, 1862.

*Ponchartrain*—Purchased at New Orleans, early 1862. Side-wheel steamer. Battery: 5 guns. Burned in Arkansas River, 1863.

*Stonewall Jackson*—Purchased at New Orleans, 1861. Side-wheel tug. Battery: 2 32-pounders. Scuttled at the fall of New Orleans.

*Tuscarora*—Purchased at New Orleans, 1861. Side-wheel steamer. Battery: 1 32-pound rifle, 1 8-inch Columbiad. Accidentally burned at New Orleans, January, 1862.

*Livingston*—Purchased at New Orleans, 1861. 180 feet long,

40 feet beam. Battery: 6 guns. Destroyed in Yazoo River, June 26, 1862.

*McRae*—Purchased at New Orleans, 1861. Screw steamer, 830 tons. Battery: 1 9-inch, 6 32-pounders. Intended as an ocean cruiser, but proved too slow. Sunk in Battle of New-Orleans.

*Webb* (formerly *William H. Webb*)—Purchased at New Orleans, 1861. Side-wheel steamer, 656 tons. 195 feet long, 31.5 feet beam. Battery: May, 1861, 4 12-pounders; February, 1863, 1 32-pounder rifle, 2 6-pounders. Remained up Arkansas River, and destroyed by Confederates on Mississippi at close of war.

All except *McRae* and *Webb* were river towboats. As originally fitted they had iron-plated ram bows for ramming, and usually a single 32-pounder forward. *Webb* was originally commissioned as a privateer.

## II. *The New Orleans Rams*

*Manassas*—Converted at Algiers, La., from tug *Enoch Train*. Ram, 387 tons. 143 feet long, 33 feet beam. Turtle-back deck of 12-inch oak and 1½-inch iron. 1 bow gun. Originally converted as a privateer by a syndicate, but her speed proving only 4 knots, she was bought by the Louisiana state government and turned over to Hollins. Sunk in action, Battle of New Orleans.

*Louisiana*—Built at New Orleans. Laid down October 15, 1861. *Virginia*-type ironclad with low ends and inclined sides. 1400 tons. 264 feet long, 62 feet beam. Two wheels in tandem amidships and two propellers, for steering. Battery: 2 9-inch and 1 7-inch rifle forward; 2 8-inch and 1 7-inch rifle astern; 1 9-inch, 2 8-inch, 7 32-pound rifles amidships. Burned after fall of New Orleans.

*Mississippi*—Ironclad ram, about 4900 tons; built at Jefferson City, La. 260 feet long, 58 feet beam. Designed for 14 knots. Three propellers. Armor: 3 inches of iron. Proposed to carry 16 heavy guns. Launched April 19, 1862, with no guns on board and burned at fall of New Orleans.

## III. Louisiana State Ships

*General Quitman*—River steamer. Battery: 2 32-pounders. Destroyed after Battle of New Orleans.

*Governor Moore*—River steamer. Battery: 2 32-pounders. Sunk in action, Battle of New Orleans.

These ships were generally similar to those of the Hollins squadron.

## IV. River Defense Fleet

These ships were seized by General Mansfield Lovell in January, 1862, and converted to rams on the lines of the Hollins vessels, with heavy double bulwarks and compressed cotton bales between. They had ram bows of 1-inch iron, and although the armament varied from time to time, it was generally 1 32-pounder forward and 1 24-pounder aft.

*Defiance*—Burned to prevent capture after Battle of New Orleans.

*General Breckinridge*—Destroyed in Battle of New Orleans.

*General Lovell*—Destroyed in Battle of New Orleans.

*Resolute*—Destroyed in Battle of New Orleans.

*Warrior*—Destroyed in Battle of New Orleans.

*Colonel Lovell*—Sunk in action, Battle of Memphis, June 6, 1862.

*General Beauregard*—Blown up in action, Battle of Memphis, June 6, 1862.

*General Bragg*—Driven ashore at Memphis, June 6, 1862, capture and taken into U.S. service. 840 tons.

*General Jeff Thompson*—Sunk in action, Battle of Memphis, June 6, 1862.

*General Sterling Price*—Disabled and driven ashore, Battle of Memphis, June 6, 1862. Raised and taken into U.S. service. 633 tons.

*General Van Dorn*—Burned by the Confederates in the Yazoo River, June 26, 1862.

*General Sumter*—Disabled and captured, Battle of Memphis,

June 6, 1862, and taken into U.S. service as *Sumter*. 400 tons.

*Little Rebel*—Disabled and captured, Battle of Memphis, June 6, 1862. Taken into U.S. service. This ship differed from the rest in being a screw steamer. 151 tons.

## V. Tennesse State Gunboat

*Eastport*—Under conversion into an ironclad at Cerro Gordo, Tenn., when captured by *Lexington, Tyler,* and *Conestoga* in February, 1862. Taken into U.S. service and completed at Cairo, Ill.

## VI. The Memphis Ironclads

*Arkansas*—Built at Memphis; towed away at approach of Union fleet and completed in the Yazoo by Lieut. I. N. Brown. Twin-screw ram of *Virginia* type. 165 feet long, 35 feet beam. Battery: 2 8-inch forward, 2 6-inch astern; 1 9-inch Dahlgren, 2 32-pound rifles, 1 6-inch on each beam. Run ashore and burned under attack by USS *Essex,* August 5, 1862, near Baton Rouge.

*Tennessee*—Duplicate of *Arkansas*. Not complete enough to be towed, therefore burned on the stocks after the Battle of Memphis, June, 1862.

## VII. The Yazoo River Ironclads

*Mobile*—Intended to be a fast ironclad screw gunboat. Construction begun at Yazoo City, but burned May, 1863, to avoid capture.

*Republic*—Duplicate of *Arkansas*. Under construction at Yazoo City, but burned to avoid capture, May, 1863.

Ironclad (unnamed)—Under construction at Yazoo City. Ram, 310 feet long, 70 feet beam, with 4½-inch armor. Four engines, with four side wheels and two propellers. Burned to avoid capture, May, 1863.

## VIII. Red River Gunboats

*Cotton* (formerly *Mary T.*)—River steamer without armor

except pressed cotton bales. Battery: 2 24-pounders, 1 small howitzer. Surrendered at Alexandria, La., June 3, 1865.

*Grand Duke*—River steamer converted at Alexandria, La., February, 1863. Oak casemate. Battery: 1 9-inch and 4 8-inch. Accidentally burned at Shreveport before January, 1864.

*Music*—Appears to have been a *Hollins*-type gunboat. There is a certain amount of mystery about this ship. No record of her exists beyond February, 1862.

## IX. Red River Ironclad

*Missouri*—Casemated stern-wheel ironclad. 183 feet long, 53 feet 8 inches beam. Armor: 4½-inch railroad iron over 23 inches of pine. Designed for 2 bow guns and 3 on each beam, but when surrendered mounted 1 11-inch, 1 9-inch, 1 32-pounder, all on pivots. Surrendered at Alexandria, La., June 3, 1865.

## B. SHIPS OF THE UNION RIVER NAVY

### I. The Rodgers Timberlads

*Conestoga*—Purchased at Cincinnati, June, 1861. Side-wheel freight steamer. 5-inch wooden armor. Battery: January, 1862, 4 32-pounders; September, 1862, 1 12-pounder rifle added; January, 1864, 3 32-pounders, 2 30-pounder Dahlgren rifles, 1 30-pounder Parrott rifle, 1 12-pounder. Sunk, March 8, 1864, by collision with *General Price*.

*Lexington*—Purchased at Cincinnati, June, 1861. Side-wheel freighter, 448 tons. 177 feet long 36 feet 10 inches beam. Speed against current 7 knots. 5-inch wooden armor. Battery: January, 1862, 4 8-inch Dahlgrens, 2 32-pounders; September, 1862. 2 30-pounder Parrott rifles added and 1 32-pounder replaced by a 12-pounder howitzer; 2 of the 8-inch Dahlgrens removed. February, 1864; 4 8-inch Dahlgrens and 1 12-pounder rifle added, September, 1864. Decommissioned July 2, 1865; sold at auction, August, 1865.

*Tyler*—Purchased at Cincinnati, June, 1861, commissioned September, 1861. Side-wheel freighter, 575 tons. 180 feet long, 45 feet 4 inches beam. Speed 8 knots against current. 5-inch wooden armor. Battery: January, 1862, 6 8-inch, 1 32-pounder; September, 1862, 3 30-pounder Parrott rifles added and 1 12-pounder substituted for the 32-pounder; March, 1864. 4 24-pounders added. Sold at auction August, 1865. Named *Taylor* by Rodgers, but this name was never officially adopted.

## II. The "Pook Turtles"

James Eads supplied the idea for these ships, but the actual design was the work of S. M. Pook. They were intended to be standard, but variations developed under construction, and further variations, especially in armament, under service conditions. The original design was for a 512-ton ship, center-wheeler, armored around the bows, with a speed of 4 knots against the current. All were built by Eads.

*Cairo*—Built at Mound City, Ill., 1861. Battery: January, 1862, 3 8-inch, 6 32-pounders, 4 42-pounder army rifles, 1 12-pounder howitzer; September, 1862, 42-pounder replaced by a 30-pounder Parrott rifle. Sunk by torpedo in the Yazoo River, December 12, 1862.

*Carondelet*—Built at St. Louis, 1861. Battery: January, 1862, 3 8-inch, 6 32-pounders, 4 42-pounder army rifles, 1 12-pounder howitzer; September, 1862, 3 of the 42-pounders replaced by 1 8-inch, 1 30-pounder rifle and 1 50-pounder rifle, while 5 of the 32-pounders were replaced by 3 9-inch; January, 1864, the remaining 32-pounder and 42-pounder were replaced by 2 100-pounder Parrott rifles; September, 1864, batter changed to 3 9-inch, 1 30-pounder and 1 50-pounder rifles and 2 100-pounder Parrotts; December, 1864, 1 12-pounder added. Sold at auction November, 1865.

*Cincinnati*—Built at Mound City, Ill., 1861. Battery: January, 1862, 3 8-inch, 6 32-pounders, 4 42-pounder army rifles, 1 12-pound howitzer; September, 1862, 2 of the 42-pounders replaced by 2 30-pounder Parrott rifles and 6 24-pound howitzers. Sunk by batteries at Vicksburg, May 27, 1863; raised, laid up at Algiers, La., and rearmed December, 1864, with 1 100-pounder Parrott rifle, 1 9-inch, 4 24-pounder howitzers. Sold out March 26, 1866.

*Louisville*—Built at St. Louis, 1861. 468 tons. Battery: January, 1862, 3 8-inch, 6 32-pounders, 4 42-pound army rifles, 1 12-pounder howitzer; September, 1862, 2 42-pounders replaced by 2 30-pounder Parrott rifles; November, 1862, 2 more 42-pounders and 1 8-inch replaced by 3 9-inch; 32-pounders removed June, 1864; November, 1864, had 1 100-pounder Parrott rifle, 4 9-inch. Sold at auction November, 1865.

*Mound City*—Built at Mound City, 1861. Undoubtedly with the usual armament of the class and of the usual dimensions. Although she took part in many actions recorded, the *Official Records* are curiously ignorant about this ship, neither listing her except in action reports nor giving any information about her disposition.

*Pittsburg*—Built at St. Louis, 1861. Battery: January, 1862, 3 9-inch, 6 32-pounders, 4 42-pounder army rifles; September, 1862, 2 42-pounders replaced by 2 30-pounder Parrott rifles and 1 12-pounder; May, 1863, 2 32-pounders replaced by 2 9-inch, 1 8-inch replaced by 1 100-pounder Parrott rifle; June, 1864, remaining 32-pounders removed. Sold at auction November, 1865.

*St. Louis* (later *Baron De Kalb*)—Built at St. Louis, 1861. Battery: January, 1862, 2 9-inch, 7 32-pounders, 4 42-pound army rifles, 1 12-pounder howitzer; September, 1862, 3 8-inch, 6 32-pounders, 2 42-pounders, 2 30-pounder rifles, 1 12-pounder howitzer; December, 1862; 2 10-inch, 2 9-inch, 6 32-pounders, 2 30-pounder rifles. Sunk by torpedo July, 1863, in Yazoo River.

### III. The Eads Ironclads

*Benton*—Converted 1861 by James B. Eads from the river wrecking ship (often called a "snag-boat") *Submarine No. 7.* Side-wheeler. Tonnage variously given between 633 and 1033.

Battery: January, 1862, 2 9-inch, 7 32-pounders, 7 42-pounder army rifles; September, 1862, 2 9-inch, 8 32-pounders, 4 42-pounder army rifles, 2 50-pounder rifles, 1 12-pounder; January, 1863, 2 additional 9-inch; as of December, 1863, 2 100-pounder Parrott rifles, 8 9-inch, 2 50-pounder rifles, 4 32-pounders. Sold at auction November, 1865.

*Essex*—Purchased September, 1861, at St. Louis for conversion; formerly center-wheel ferryboat *New Era*, built St. Louis, 1856. Tonnage variously given in official records as 355 and 614. Battery: January, 1862, 1 10-inch, 3 9-inch, 1 32-pounder, 1 12-pounder howitzer; September, 1862; 12-pounder howitzer replaced by a 24-pounder, 2 50-pounder rifles added; June, 1863, 1 100-pounder Parrott rifle, 1 32-pounder Parrott rifle, 2 50-pounder rifles, 4 9-inch, 1 12-pounder rifle, 3 12-pounder: January, 1864, 2 100-pounder Parrott rifles, 6 9-inch, 1 12-pounder rifle, 3 12-pounders. Sold at auction November, 1865.

## *IV. The Porter Ironclads*

These ships were built at St. Louis by Eads under the design of Commander W. D. Porter, and whose authority no one has ever been able to discover.

*Choctaw*—Built at St. Louis, 1862. Side-wheel ironclad, 1004 tons. Speed against current 2 knots. Battery: June, 1862, 3 9-inch, 2 30-pounder Parrott rifles, 2 24-pounders; January, 1863, 1 100-pounder Parrott rifle added; April, 1863, 2 of the 9-inch removed but restored September, 1863, and the 24-pounders replaced by 12-pounders. Sold out March, 1866.

*Lafayette* (formerly *Fort Henry*)—Built at St. Louis, 1862. 1000 tons. 280 feet long, 45 feet beam. Battery: February, 1863, 2 11-inch, 4 9-inch, 2 100-pound Parrott rifles; April, 1863, 4 24-pounder howitzers added; May, 1863, 2 of the 24-pounder replaced by 12-pounders. Sold out March, 1866.

## *V. The Cincinnati Ironclads*

These ships were built at Cincinnati by Joseph Brown to plans by an unknown designer. (*See text.*)

*Chillicothe*—Completed October, 1862. Side-wheeler, 395 tons. 162 feet long. Battery: 2 11-inch, 1 12-pounder. Sold out November, 1865.

*Indianola*—Built 1862. Side-wheels and screw, 511 tons. Speed against current 6 knots. Battery: 2 11-inch, 2 9-inch. Captured February, 1863, and scuttled by Confederates. Subsequently raised by Union forces and sold at auction, 1865.

*Tuscumbia*—Launched December 2, 1862, at New Albany, Ind. Commissioned March, 1863. Side-wheel and screw, 915 tons. Battery: 3 11-inch, 2 9-inch. Sold at auction November, 1865.

## VI. The River Monitors

*Neosho*—Built at St. Louis by Eads. Commissioned May 13. 1863. Stern-wheel single turret, 523 tons. Battery: 2 11-inch, 1 12-pounder; March, 1864, 1 12-pounder rifle on deck added. Out of commission July 23, 1865. Name changed to *Vixen* 1869, then to *Osceola*. Sold out 1873.

*Osage*—Built at St. Louis by Eads. Commissioned July 10, 1863. 523 tons. Speed against current 7.5 knots. Battery: 2 11-inch; January, 1864, 1 12-pounder rifle on deck added. Sunk by torpedo in Blakely River, Ala., raised and sold at auction 1867.

*Ozark*—Built at Mound City by George C. Bestor. Commissioned February, 1864. Unlike the two previous of the class she was a twin-screw ship, with a speed of 2.5 knots against current. Battery: 2 11-inch, 1 12-pounder rifle; 1 10-inch on deck added July, 1864, and 3 9-inch later. Sold out November, 1865.

*Marietta*—Built at Pittsburgh by Tomlinson, Hartupee & Co. Completed 1864. Single screw, 479 tons. 170 feet long, 50 feet beam. Single turret. Battery: 2 11-inch. Name changed to *Circe* and back to *Marietta*, 1869. Sold out 1873.

*Sandusky*—Sister ship to *Marietta;* built at Pittsburgh by same firm. Launched January, 1865. Name changed to *Minerva* and back, 1869. Sold out 1873.

*Catawba*—Built by Niles Works, Cincinnati. Screw single-turret monitor, 1034 tons. Length 235 feet, beam 46 feet. Battery: 2 15-inch. Delivered June 7, 1865. Probably sold out 1873.

*Tippecanoe*—Sister ship to *Catawba*. Built at Cincinnati by Miles Greenwood. Completed 1865. Name changed to *Vesuvius* and then to *Wyandotte,* 1869. Probably sold out 1873.

*Chickasaw*—Built at St. Loius by T. G. Gaylord; delivered May, 1864. Double-turret screw monitor with turtle-back deck, one Eads and one Ericsson turret. 970 tons. Length 257 feet, beam 57 feet. Battery: 4 11-inch. Name changed to *Samson* and back, 1869. Sold out 1874.

*Winnebago*—Built at St. Louis by Eads. Launched July 4, 1863. Sister ship to *Chickasaw*. Name changed to *Tornado* and back, 1869. Sold out 1874.

*Kickapoo*—Built at St. Louis by G. B. Allen & Co. Commissioned July 8, 1864. Sister ship to *Chickasaw*. Name changed to *Cyclone* and then *Kewaydin,* 1869. Sold out 1874.

*Milwaukee*—Built at St. Louis by Eads. Delivered August 2, 1864. Sister ship to *Chickasaw*. Sunk by torpedo in Blakely River, Ala., March 20, 1865.

## VII. The Ellet Rams

As originally built these wooden rams carried no armament but the small arms of the crew, though later in the war many were supplied with 24-pound howitzers. *(See text.)*

*Lancaster*—Side-wheeler, 350 tons. Sunk by Vicksburg batteries, March 25, 1863.

*Mingo*—Stern-wheeler, 300 tons. Bought and converted at Pittsburgh. Speed against current 12 knots. Accidentally sunk at Cape Girardeau, Mo., November, 1862.

*Lioness*—Stern-wheeler, 300 tons. Bought and converted at Pittsburgh.

*Monarch*—Side-wheeler, 400 tons. Bought at Cincinnati.

*Dick Fulton*—Stern-wheeler, 175 tons. Bought at Pittsburgh.

*Queen of the West*—Side-wheeler, 400 tons. Bought at Cincinnati. Grounded in Red River and captured by Confederates, February 14, 1863.

*Samson*—Stern-wheeler, 300 tons. Bought at Pittsburgh. Sold out August, 1865.

*Switzerland*—Side-wheeler, 400 tons. Bought at Cincinnati. Sunk by Vicksburg batteries March 25, 1863.

*T. D. Horner*—Stern-wheeler, 200 tons. Bought at Pittsburgh.

## VIII. Confederate Ships Captured

*Robb*—Wooden gunboat, captured April 19, 1862, at Florence, Ala., by *Tyler*. Stern-wheeler; 86 tons. 114 feet 9 inches long, 20 feet beam. Speed 9.5 knots against the current. Battery: 2 12-pounder rifles, 2 12-pounders; 1 20-pounder Parrott added February, 1865. Sold out August, 1865.

*Eastport*—Ironclad gunboat, captured while incomplete at Cerro Gordo, Tenn., February 7, 1862, and completed at Mound City. 700 tons. Battery: October, 1862, 4 32-pounders, 2 30-pounder Parrott rifles, 2 50-pounder rifles, 2 12-pounder rifles; January, 1863, changed to 6 9-inch, 2 100-pounder Parrott rifles; July, 1863, 2 of the 9-inch replaced by 50-pounder Dahlgren rifles. Badly damaged by torpedo in Red River April 26, 1864, and blown up by Admiral Porter.

*General Bragg*—Captured, Battle of Memphis, June 6, 1862. Side-wheeler, 840 tons. Speed 10 knots against current. Battery: 1 30-pounder Parrott rifle, 1 32-pounder, 1 12-pounder rifle. Sold out July, 1865.

*General Pillow*—Captured June, 1862, near Fort Pillow by *Pittsburg*, as *B. M. Moore*, an unarmed steamer. Side-wheeler, 38 tons. Battery: 2 12-pound howitzers. Sold out November, 1865.

*General Price*—Sunk, Battle of Memphis, June 6, 1862; raised and taken into Union service. Side-wheeler, 633 tons. Battery: March, 1863, 4 9-inch; May, 1863, 2 9-inch removed and 1 12-pounder added; October, 1864, 1 12-pounder rifle added. Sold out October, 1865.

*Little Rebel*—Captured, Battle of Memphis, June 6, 1862. Screw, 151 tons. Battery, September, 1862; 2 12-pounder rifles; March, 1863, 2 24-pounder howitzers added. Sold out November, 1865.

*Sumter* (formerly *C S S General Sumter*)—Captured, Battle of Memphis, June 6, 1862. 400 tons. Battery: 2 32-pounders. Grounded and abandoned off Bayou Sara, August, 1862. Subsequently burned by Confederates.

*Alexandria* (formerly *C S S St. Mary*)—Captured, Yazoo City, July 13, 1863. Altered and commissioned at Cairo, December, 1863. Side-wheeler, 60 tons. Battery: 1 24-pounder, 1 12-pounder. Sold out August, 1865.

*Tensas* (formerly Confederate unarmed steamer *Tom Sugg*) —Captured August 14, 1863, in Little Red River by *Cricket*. Side-wheeler, 41 tons. 91 feet 8 inches long, 22 feet 5 inches beam. Speed 4 knots against current. Battery: 2 24-pounder howitzers. Sold out August, 1865.

*Volunteer*—Unarmed steamer seized November 25, 1863, by *Fort Hindman,* while in possession of army troops illegally loading cotton near Natchez Island. Condemned as prize and purchased by navy, February, 1864. Stern-wheeler, 209 tons. Speed against current 6 knots. Battery: 1 12-pounder. Sold out November, 1865.

## IX. Tinclads, 1862

*Black Hawk*—Purchased at Cairo, November, 1862. Sidewheeler, 902 tons. Battery: May, 1863, 4 32-pounders, 2 30-pounder Parrott rifles, 1 12-pounder, 1 12-pounder rifle; February, 1864, 32-pounders replaced by 8 23-pounders and another 12-pounder rifle added. Accidentally blown up and sunk in Ohio River near Cairo, April 22, 1865. Raised and sold by wrecking firm, 1867. Command ship.

*Brilliant*—Purchased at St. Louis, August 13, 1862. Sidewheeler, 226 tons. Speed 6 knots against current. Battery: September, 1862, 2 12-pounder rifles, 2 12-pounder; February, 1863, 2 24-pounders added. Sold out August, 1865.

*Cricket*—Purchased at Cincinnati, November 15, 1862.

Stern-wheeler, 178 tons. Battery: January, 1863, 6 24-pound howitzers; August, 1864, 2 20-pounder rifles, 4 24-pounder howitzers, 1 12-pounder. Sold out August, 1864.

*Curlew*—Purchased at Cincinnati, December 17, 1862. Stern-wheeler, 196 tons. Speed against current 4 knots. Battery: 6 32-pounders, 1 20-pounder Parrott rifle; February, 1863, 8 24-pounder howitzers. Sold out August, 1865.

*Estrella*—Transferred 1862 from army command. Side-wheeler, 438 tons. Battery: 1 30-pounder Parrott rifle, 2 32-pounders, 2 24-pounder howitzers. Sold out October, 1867.

*Fairplay*—Transferred September, 1862, from army command. Side-wheeler, 156 tons. Battery: September, 1862, 2 12-pounder howitzers, 2 12-pounder rifles; May, 1863, 1 32-pounder, 2 12-pounder howitzers, 4 12-pounder rifles; October, 1863, 32-pounder replaced by 30-pounder Parrott rifle; March, 1864, another 30-pounder Parrott rifle added. Sold out August, 1865.

*Forest Rose*—Purchased at Cincinnati November 5, 1862. Stern-wheeler, 260 tons. Speed against current 6 knots. Battery: 2 30-pounder Parrott rifles, 4 24-pounder howitzers; August, 1863, 2 32-pounders added. Sold out August, 1865.

*Glide*—Purchased at Pittsburgh, November 30, 1862. Side-wheeler, 232 tons. Battery: 2 32-pounders, 4 24-pounder howitzers. Sold out August, 1865.

*Great Western*—Transferred from army command, September 30, 1862. Side-wheeler, 800 tons. Battery: 1 32-pounder, 1 12-pounder, 1 6-pounder rifle. Sold out November, 1865. (There is no explanation of why so large a ship carried so small a battery.)

*Judge Torrence*—Transferred from army command, September 30, 1862. Side-wheeler, 700 tons. Speed against current 7 knots. Battery: 2 24-pound howitzers, 1 12-pound howitzer, 1 6-pounder rifle. Sold out August, 1865.

*Juliet*—Purchased at Cincinnati, November 1, 1862. Stern-wheeler, 157 tons. Speed 4 knots against current. Battery: 6 24-pounder howitzers. Sold out August, 1865.

*Linden*—Purchased at Cincinnati, November 20, 1862. Side-wheeler, 177 tons. Battery: 6 24-pounder howitzers. Sunk on snag in Arkansas River, February 22, 1864.

*Marmora*—Purchased at St. Louis, September 17, 1862; commissioned October 21. Stern-wheeler, 207 tons. Speed against current 6 knots. Battery: December, 1862, 2 24-pounders, 2 12-pounder rifles; June, 1864, added 4 24-pounders. Sold out July, 1865.

*New Era*—Purchased at Cincinnati, October 27, 1862. Stern-wheeler, 157 tons. Battery: 6 24-pounder howitzers. Sold out June, 1865.

*Petrel*—Purchased at Cincinnati, December 22, 1862. 226 tons. Battery: 8 24-pounder howitzers. Captured and destroyed by batteries in the Yazoo River, April 30, 1864.

*Prairie Bird* (formerly *Mary Miller*)—Purchased at Cincinnati, December 19, 1862. Stern-wheeler, 177 tons. Speed 6 knots against current. Battery: 8 24-pounder howitzers. Sold out August, 1865.

*Rattler* (formerly *Florence Miller*)—Purchased at Cincinnati, November 11, 1862. Stern-wheeler, 165 tons. Battery: 2 30-pounder Parrott rifles, 2 24-pounders; January, 1864, 2 more 24-pounders added. Run ashore and abandoned near Grand Gulf, December 30, 1864.

*Romeo*—Purchased at Cincinnati, October 31, 1862. Stern-wheeler, 175 tons. Speed against current 5 knots. Battery: 6 24-pounder howitzers. Sold out August, 1865.

*St. Clair*—Purchased at St. Louis, August 12, 1862, commissioned September 24. Stern-wheeler, 203 tons. Battery: September, 1862, 2 12-pounders, 2 12-pounder rifles; February, 1863, 2 24-pounder howitzers; May, 1863, 2 24-pounder howitzers, 2 12-pounders, 1 12-pounder rifle; December, 1863, 1 12-pounder rifle added; December, 1864, 2 50-pounder rifles, 4 24-pounder howitzers, 2 12-pounders. Sold out August, 1865.

*Signal*—Purchased at St. Louis, September 25, 1862. Stern-wheeler, 190 tons. Battery: January, 1863, 2 30-pounder Parrott rifles, 4 24-pounder howitzers, 2 12-pounder rifles; February, 1864; 30-pounder rifles replaced by 2 32-pounders. Sunk by shore batteries in Red River, May 5, 1864.

*Springfield* (formerly *W. A. Healy*)—Purchased at Cincinnati, November 20, 1862. Stern-wheeler, 146 tons. Speed against current 5 knots. Battery: 6 24-pounder howitzers. Sold out August, 1865.

## X. Tinclads, 1863

*Argosy*—Purchased at Cairo, March 24, 1863. Stern-wheeler, 219 tons. Speed against current 5 knots. Battery: March, 1863, 6 24-pounders, 2 12-pounder rifles; January, 1864, 2 12-pounders added, 1 12-pounder rifle removed. Sold out August, 1865.

*Avenger*—Built for the army at New Albany, Ind., 1863. Side-wheeler with ram, 410 tons. Speed 11 knots. Battery: September, 1863, 1 100-pounder Parrott rifle, 1 12-pounder rifle, 4 24-pounders; December, 1863, 1 24-pounder added. Sold out November, 1865.

*Champion*—Purchased at Cincinnati, March 24, 1863. Side-wheeler, 115 tons. Speed against current 4 knots. Battery: November, 1863, 2 30-pounder Parrott rifles, 1 24-pounder, 2 12-pounder howitzers; December, 1864, 2 30-pounder Parrott rifles, 2 24-pounder, 4 12-pounder rifles. Sold out September, 1865.

*Covington*—Purchased at Cairo, March 9, 1863. Side-wheeler, 224 tons. Battery: 4 24-pounders, 2 30-pounder Parrott rifles, 2 50-pounder rifles; March, 1865, 1 12-pounder added. Sunk in Red River by shore batteries, May 5, 1864.

*Elk* (formerly *Countess*)—Purchased at Cincinnati, December 8, 1863. Side-wheeler, 162 tons. Battery: 2 32-pounders, 4 24-pounders. Sold out August, 1865.

*Exchange*—Purchased at Cincinnati, May 13, 1863. Stern-wheeler, 211 tons. Speed against current 6 knots. Battery: 2 32-pounders, 4 24-pounders, 1 12-pounder rifle. Sold out August, 1865.

*Fawn* (formerly *Fanny Barker*)—Purchased at Cincinnati, May 13, 1863. Stern-wheeler, 174 tons. Speed against current

4 knots. Battery: 6 24-pounder howitzers; March, 1864, add 1 12-pounder rifle; December, 1864, add 1 24-pounder howitzer. Sold out August, 1865.

*Fort Hindman* (formerly *James Thompson*) —Purchased at Jeffersonville, Ind., April 13, 1863. Side-wheeler, 288 tons. Battery: 6 8-inch; December, 1863, add 1 12-pounder howitzer; June, 1864, add 1 100-pounder Parrott rifle; December, 1864, add 1 12-pounder rifle. Name changed to *Manitou*, then back to *Fort Hindman*.

*Gazelle* (formerly *Emma Brown*) —Purchased at Cincinnati, November 21, 1863. Side-wheeler, 117 tons. Speed against current 5 knots. Battery: 6 12-pounder rifles. Sold out August, 1865.

*Hastings* (formerly *Emma Duncan*) —Purchased at Cairo, March 24, 1863. Side-wheeler, 293 tons. Battery: 2 30-pounder Parrott rifles, 2 32-pounders, 4 24-pounders; April, 1864, add 1 12-pounder. Sold out July, 1865.

*Kenwood*—Purchased at Cincinnati, commissioned May 24, 1863, at Cairo. Stern-wheeler, 232 tons. Battery: 2 32-pounders, 4 24-pounder howitzers; December, 1863, 32-pounders replaced by 2 30-pounder Parrott rifles and 2 12-pounders; June, 1864, add 2 12-pounder howitzers. Sold out August, 1865.

*Key West*—Purchased at Cairo, commissioned May 26, 1863. Stern-wheeler, 207 tons. Battery: 6 24-pounder howitzers, 2 24-pounders, 1 12-pounder rifle. Sunk in action in the Tennessee River, November 4, 1864.

*Moose* (formerly *Florence Miller*) —Purchased at Cincinnati. Stern-wheeler, 189 tons. Speed against current, 6 knots. Battery: June, 1863, 6 24-pounders; May, 1864: add 2 20-pounder rifles, 2 12-pounders. Sold out August, 1865.

*Naumkeag*—Purchased at Cairo, commissioned April 16, 1863. Stern-wheeler, 148 tons. Speed against current 6 knots. Battery: 2 30-pounder Parrott rifles, 4 24-pounders; December, 1864, add 1 12-pounder. Sold out August, 1865.

*Nyanza*—Purchased at Cincinnati, commissioned December 21, 1863. Side-wheeler, 203 tons. Battery: 6 24-pound howitzers; June, 1864, add 2 20-pounder Parrott rifles. Sold out August, 1865.

*Ouachita* (formerly *Louisville*) —Purchased at Cairo, September 29, 1863, commissioned January 18, 1864. Side-wheeler, 720 tons. Battery: 5 30-pounder Parrott rifles, 18 24-pounders, 15 12-pounders, 1 12-pounder rifle. Sold out September, 1865.

*Paw Paw* (formerly *St. Charles*) —Missouri River steamer, purchased at Chicago, April, 1863. Center-wheeler, 175 tons. Speed against current 4 knots. Battery: 2 30-pounder Parrott rifles, 6 24-pounder howitzers. Sold out July, 1865.

*Peosta*—Purchased June 13, 1863, at Dubuque, Ia., commissioned October 2. Side-wheeler, 233 tons. Speed against current 5 knots. Battery: 3 30-pounder Parrott rifles, 3 32-pounders, 6 24-pound howitzers, 2 12-pounders. Sold out August, 1865.

*Queen City*—Purchased February 12, 1863, at Cincinnati, commissioned April 1. Side-wheeler, 212 tons. Battery: 2 30-pounder Parrott rifles, 2 32-pounders, 4 24-pound howitzers; October, 1863, add 1 12-pounder. Destroyed June 12, 1864, at Clarendon, Ark.

*Reindeer* (formerly *Rachel Miller*)—Purchased at Cincinnati, June 13, 1863, commissioned July 25. Stern-wheeler, 212 tons. Speed against current 8 knots. Battery: 6 24-pound howitzers; March, 1865, add 2 30-pounder Parrott rifles. Sold out August, 1865.

*Silver Cloud*—Purchased at Cairo, May 19, 1863. Stern-wheeler, 236 tons. Speed against current 6 knots. Battery: 6 24-pounder howitzers; September, 1864, add 1 24-pounder rifle. Sold out August, 1865.

*Stockdale*—Purchased at Cincinnati, November 13, 1863. Side-wheeler, 188 tons. Battery: 2 30-pounder Parrott rifles, 4 24-pounder howitzers. Sold out August, 1865.

*Tawah*—Purchased at St. Joseph, Mo., June 10, 1863. Side-wheeler, 108 tons. Battery: 2 30-pounder Parrott rifles, 4 24-pounders, 1 12-pounder, 1 12-pounder rifle. Sunk and burned at Johnsonville in the Tennessee, November 4, 1864.

*Victory* (formerly *Bunker*)—Purchased at Cincinnati, commissioned July 8, 1863. Stern-wheeler, 160 tons. Speed against current 5 knots. Battery: 6 24-pounder howitzers. Sold out August, 1865.

*Wave*—Purchased at Cincinnati, November 14, 1863. Side-wheeler, 229 tons. Battery: 6 24-pounder howitzers. Captured May 6, 1864, at Calcasieu Pass, Tex.

## XI. Tinclads, 1864

*Carrabasset*—Purchased at Cincinnati, January 23, 1864. Side-wheeler, 202 tons. Battery: 2 32-pounders, 4 24-pounders. Sold out August, 1865.

*Collier* (formerly *Allen Collier*)—Purchased at Cincinnati (date not recorded). Battery: 2 30-pounder Parrott rifles, 1 12-pounder, 6 24-pounder howitzers. Sold out August, 1865.

*Colossus*—Purchased at Cincinnati, December 8, 1864. Stern-wheeler, 183 tons. Speed against current 5 knots. Battery: 2 30-pounder Parrott rifles, 4 24-pounders. Sold out August 1865.

*Elfin*—Purchased at Cincinnati, February 23, 1864. 192 tons. Battery: 8 24-pounder howitzers. Sunk at Johnsonville in the Tennessee, November 4, 1864.

*Fairy* (formerly *Maria*)—Purchased March 7, 1864. Stern-wheeler, 211 tons. Speed against current 5.5 knots. Battery: 2 30-pounder Parrott rifles, 6 24-pounder howitzers. Sold out August, 1865.

*Gamage* (formerly *Willie Gamage*)—Purchased at Cincinnati, December 24, 1864. Side-wheeler, 187 tons. Battery: 6 24-pounder howitzers, 2 20-pounder Parrott rifles, 1 12-pounder rifle. Sold out August, 1865.

*Grosbeak* (formerly *Fanny*)—Purchased at Cincinnati, February 3, 1864. Side-wheeler, 196 tons. Battery: 2 30-pounder Parrott rifles, 2 20-pounder Parrott rifles, 2 24-pounders, 1 12-pounder. Sold out August, 1865.

*Huntress*—Purchased at Louisville, June 9, 1864. Stern-wheeler, 211 tons. Speed against current 6 knots. Battery:

2 30-pounder Parrott rifles, 4 24-pounder howitzers. Sold out August, 1865.

*Ibex* (formerly *Ohio Valley*) —Purchased at Cincinnati, December 16, 1864. Side-wheeler, 235 tons. Battery: 2 30-pounder Parrott rifles, 2 12-pounder rifles, 4 24-pounder howitzers. Sold out August, 1865.

*Kate* (formerly *Kate B. Porter*)—Purchased at Cincinnati, December 23, 1864, commissioned April 2, 1865. Stern-wheeler, 242 tons. Speed against current 6 knots. Battery: 2 20-pounder Parrott rifles, 6 24-pounder howitzers, 2 12-pounder howitzers. Sold out March, 1866.

*Meteor* (formerly *Sciota*)—Purchased at Cincinnati, January 23, 1864. Side-wheeler, 221 tons. Battery: 2 32-pounders, 4 24-pounders; October, 1864, 32-pounders replaced by 2 30-pounder Parrott rifles. Sold out September, 1865.

*Naiad* (formerly *Princess*) —Purchased at Cincinnati, March 3, 1864. Stern-wheeler, 183 tons. Speed against current 6 knots. Battery: 8 24-pounders; December, 1864, 2 30-pounder Parrott rifles, 6 24-pounders. Sold out August, 1865.

*Nymph* (formerly *Cricket No. 2*) —Purchased at Cincinnati, March 8, 1864, commissioned April 11. Stern-wheeler, 171 tons. Speed against current 4 knots. Battery: 8 24-pounders, 4 24-pounder howitzers. Sold out August, 1865.

*Oriole* (formerly *Florence Miller*) —Purchased at Cincinnati, December 7, 1864. 137 tons. Battery: 2 30-pounder Parrott rifles, 6 24-pounder howitzers, 1 12-pounder rifle. Sold out August, 1865.

*Peri* (formerly *Reindeer*) —Purchased at Cincinnati, April 30, 1864, commissioned June 20. Stern-wheeler, 209 tons. Speed against current 6 knots. Battery: 2 30-pounder Parrott rifles, 6 24-pounders. Sold out August, 1865.

*Rodolph*—Purchased at Cincinnati, December 31, 1863, commissioned May 28, 1864. Side-wheeler, 217 tons. Battery: 2 32-pounders, 4 24-pounder howitzers; August, 1864, 32-pounders replaced by 2 30-pounder Parrott rifles. Sunk by torpedo in Blakely River, Ala., April 1, 1865.

*Sibyl* (formerly *Hartford*)—Purchased at Cincinnati, April 27, 1864, commissioned June 16. Side-wheeler, 176 tons. Battery: 2 30-pounder Parrott rifles, 4 24-pounders; September, 1864, add 2 24-pounders. Sold out August, 1865.

*Siren* (formerly *White Rose*)—Purchased at Cincinnati, March 11, 1864, commissioned August 30. Stern-wheeler, 214 tons. Speed against current 7 knots. Battery: 2 30-pounder Parrott rifles, 6 24-pounder howitzers. Sold out August, 1865.

*Tallahatchie* (formerly *Cricket No. 1*)—Purchased at Cincinnati, January 23, 1864, commissioned April 19. Side-wheeler, 171 tons. Battery: 2 32-pounders, 4 24-pounder howitzers. Sold out August, 1865.

*Undine* (formerly *Ben Gaylord*)—Purchased at Cincinnati, March 7, 1864. 179 tons. Battery: 8 24-pounder howitzers. Captured October 30, 1864, in the Tennessee River and burned November 4.

*Vindicator*—Built for army at New Albany, Ind., transferred to navy and commissioned May 24, 1864. Side-wheel ram, 400 tons. Speed against current 12 knots. Battery: 1 100-pounder Parrott rifle, 2 24-pounder howitzers, 2 12-pounder rifles; December, 1864, add 1 30-pounder Parrott rifle and 8 24-pounders. Sold out November, 1865.

## XII. Tennessee River Gunboats

These ships were built by the army at Chattanooga for Tennessee River service, commissioned in July, 1864, and transferred to the navy.

*General Burnside*—Side-wheeler, 201 tons. Battery: 2 20-pounder Parrott rifles, 3 24-pounder howitzers.

*General Grant*—Sister-ship to the above, of same dimensions and armament.

*General Sherman*—Side-wheeler, 187 tons. Same armament as *General Burnside*.

*General Thomas*—Side-wheeler, 184 tons. Battery: 2 20-pounder Parrott rifles, 4 24-pounder howitzers.

All four ships returned to army authority, June 1, 1865.

# Index